Basics for Scholastic Chess Players:

A Guide for Players and Coaches

Leonard S. Dickerson

March 31, 2011

Table of Contents

Introduction

With new things constantly arresting my attention, republishing this book was a rare opportunity that I got. Many authors wish that they had the time to refine a previous work. I was able to do this and feel blessed to have been able to do so. Updating this book was a joy, mainly because I was able to correct many oversights that the first book contained as well as add new developments that have unfolded since the publication of my first edition over 11 years ago.

Nationwide scholastic chess participation continues at a record pace and grows yearly. In Tennessee, scholastic team chess has grown over 600% since 1989. During this growth period, I have been actively engaged in teaching chess players and developing scholastic chess programs in the school system. I am often asked what the requirements are for a player to be considered good enough to represent the school in team play. This book is being written to offer scholastic programs – including colleges and universities – a basis for qualifying their players for team competition.

This manual contains the material which I have found to be essential in assuring that players are adequately prepared to competitively play and advance in chess, later educating themselves through practice and more advanced study based on the proper groundwork having been laid early in their development. The goal is not to produce superior players who are booked-up but simply to produce good scholastic players who have the fundamental knowledge to play equally with their peers. The material to be mastered is not difficult nor particularly comprehensive. (In fact, the total coverage could easily be presented within a 5-week course.) However, it is inclusive of all the elements which experience and practice have indicated are necessary for scholastic achievement.

As an example of the practicalness of the material, consider that the Scholars' Mate is detailed in this manual! Now I certainly am not presenting the Scholars' Mate in hopes that students will attempt to play it. Heavens no! I want to demystify it to the beginner and expose it as a weak attempt which should not be feared and which will often boomerang on the perpetrator. It is presented here because it is so prevalent at the scholastic level. No one should be considered for team competition unless they are familiar with it and know how to counter its attempt. I've seen too many children and chess coordinators devastated by this ancient mate spoiling a school's chance for championship qualification.

I've also seen many coaches and parents disappointed that their well-coached kid who has been trained to work 4-move combinations still commits one-move blunders while under no pressure. This manual will not cure that ill by itself. (However, in the Appendix there is a comprehensive methodology for error reduction that certainly will reduce one-move blunders. It is another book of itself, though!) This manual presents what it takes for the coach to equip the student with the required knowledge to be skillful. It is still up to the chess coach and student to demonstrate excellence in application of the knowledge.

Hence this practical presentation won't focus on performing three- and four-move combinations. It focuses on seeing the next move. I've learned from experience and years of teaching that if one can simply lessen the number of one-move blunders that their players commit that their team will then have a good shot at the state championship! Hence I look at practical material addressing the goal of diminishing blunders rather than directly increasing tactical ability.

Because the explosive growth of chess is almost overwhelming, many scholastic programs are nearly paralyzed by huge classes of 50 or more students who have varying degrees of interest and skill. Some students simply want to have fun, some may be competitive, and some may just want to socialize! Our goal as coaches of this hodgepodge is to present them what they need to play a good game and to develop further in chess as they wish. Practice and interest will hone their skill after the base has been built.

Leonard S. Dickerson,
National Chess Master
3-time Tenn. Chess Champion
March 31, 2011

Foreword

It is my hope that students and coaches will start from Section 1 and work through to the end of the book. However, the essential material for players to learn to assure that they are ready to compete in scholastic tournaments can be taught from this book during five periods of two hours duration. I will later specify exactly what those sections are while detailing their importance.

I have organized the book with the present layout because it is the logical manner in which I have taught several chess courses: (1) introduce the students to the value of the pieces and their moves; (2) present them with enough basic knowledge to start playing chess games because they will be impatient to start play – even if they don't know how the pieces move; (3) teach them some basic mates so that they can more efficiently conclude their games; (4) introduce candidate move selection and stress ways of avoiding one-move blunders before moving on to combinations; and (5) teach them the more involved chess endings that they will begin to encounter more frequently when their opponents stop committing suicide and leaving them with piece-up endgames to play. The reason that I placed openings before learning basic mates is that I have taught many classes of 40 or more children and have discovered that they are so antsy to play that they won't retain mating instruction until they personally see why they need to know it. If you are teaching 10 or less students, I would advise presenting a lesson on mating before dwelling on openings.

Observe that even though I present endgames last, their presentation takes up the most pages. Endgames and combinations (tactical play) is where the beginning student's focus should be – not openings. Give students only enough opening instruction so that they can properly develop their pieces. We are not trying to win openings. We are trying to show students how to win games.

The material that is designated as *Advancing in Chess* can be skipped in your initial coverage. This material is for students who want to acquire more than just the basics and is recommended for anyone who plans to play chess seriously. The book recommendations can be particularly useful for self-study and advancement. Book recommendations have been arranged in order of their user-friendliness or usefulness for establishing a basis for more challenging material. While some of the books are dated, the ideas are very applicable to skill development and current tournament play. It is recommended, though, that you seek to purchase the latest version of the books that have been published and use my sketchy bibliographical information only as reference.

Also, the material in the Appendix can be skipped initially. It serves to supplement the main sections without bogging the new student down with so much detail that the message could be obscured. The usefulness of the material in the Appendix depends greatly upon the student's continued and active interest.

If you are simply a parent or new chess player seeking to improve your skill and determine what basic knowledge you need to become a decent chess player, then you can skip Section VII, *Team Play*. On the other hand, chess coaches or chess team coordinators (especially those who participate in the Tennessee scholastics) should consider Section VII a must read, particularly *Team Specifics in Tennessee*, which contains guidelines about Alternate substitution and B Teams.

This book is based on the premise that there is specific knowledge with which all fair scholastic chess players are familiar, and those who aspire to represent the school or club should be expected to be able to demonstrate this knowledge. This knowledge can be introduced to most students over a 10-hour period. Though the material can be introduced quickly, you still need to allow the student time to assimilate the topics and later demonstrate their understanding in games or by testing.

A listing of the elements that the players need to have mastered if they plan to represent the school or club are listed below with the reference section in which the information is contained. The following items must be mastered before one will be considered to be eligible to represent in tournament competition:

• Know the point value of all the chess pieces. [Sect. 1, **p. 1**]

• Know what the Scholars' Mate is and how to avoid it when playing
     Black. [Sect. 2, **pp. 25-31**]

• Know how to promote a pawn to a queen or other piece.
     [Sect. I, **p. 4**; Sect. VI, **pp. 81-85**]

• Know what the opposition is and how to use it for pawn promotion
     [Sect. VI, **pp. 86-89**]

- Know what taking a pawn *en-passant* (in passing) means.
  [Sect. I, **pp. 5**]

- Know how to keep score. [Sect. 1, **pp. 7-10**; Sect. VII, **p. 107–108**]

- Demonstrate good opening play, developing pieces and castling early.
  [Sect. II, **pp. 17-22**]

- Know the king-rook mate and be able to execute it within 40 moves.
  [Sect. III, **pp. 41-43**]

- Know the difference between stalemate and checkmate. [Sect. III, **p. 47-48**]

- Know what the 50-move drawing rule means.
  [Sect. III, **pp. 46-47 & 50**]

- Know what a draw by three-fold repetition of position means.
  [Sect. III, **p. 46 & 49**]

- Know what a draw by insufficient mating chances means.
  [Sect. III, **p. 46 &49**; Sect. VII, **p. 107**]

- Know where rooks belong to either promote one's own or stop the
  opponent's pawns. [Sect. VI, **pp. 82-83**]

- Be familiar enough with a chess clock so that its use does not distract
  from one's play. [Sect. VII, **pp. 103-104**]

- Play touch-move chess. [Sect. VII, **p. 108**]

- Keep quiet while chess games are ongoing – yours or others.
  [Sect. VII, **p. 104–105**]

I. The Chessboard and Pieces

The Pieces' Value and Movement

The Pieces and Their Value		
Piece	Symbol	Value
King	K (♔)	Game*
Queen	Q (♕)	9
Rook	R (♖)	5
Bishop	B (♗)	3
Knight	N (♘)	3
Pawn	P (♙)	1

*Assigning the value *game* to the king means that the king is invaluable or worth the whole game. It is worth any amount of material to protect or sacrifice for the king because capture of the king ends the game.

The moves of the pieces are illustrated on the following page. Before we get into specific moves of the pieces, there are some definitions (*Definitions*, in general, at are back of the book) and characteristics of piece movement with which we need to become acquainted:

Captures are made by removing the opponent's man from a square and replacing it with the capturing man. All captures are optional except when necessary to avoid checkmate.

Check or Checkmate occurs when the king is being directly attacked—or checked—by a piece. If the king cannot remove himself from check, then he is checkmated—the object of the game. The king must remove itself from check, if possible, and can never place itself in check.

1

Moves of the pieces: In the diagrams below, the " ∗ " represents the squares where the pieces can legally move and capture – except for the pawn, which moves (denoted by " ● ") differently from its captures.

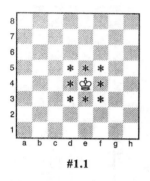

#1.1

The king can be moved to any square adjoining the square he occupies. He captures any unprotected opposing man in the same manner that he moves.

#1.2

The pawn moves forward only one square at a time – except on its first move where each has the option of moving two squares. It captures diagonally one space on adjacent squares, denoted as " ∗ ".

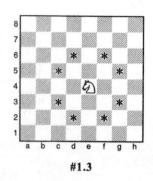

#1.3

The knight moves and captures in any direction by moving in small "L-shaped" configurations of "1-2 squares" or " 2-1 squares." It can jump over its own pieces.

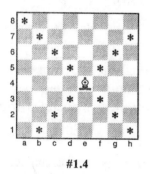

#1.4

The bishop moves and captures diagonally in any direction over unoccupied squares.

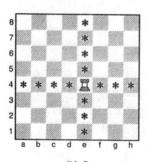

#1.5

The rook moves and captures on the rank (horizontally) and file (vertically) over unoccupied squares.

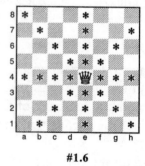

#1.6

The queen moves like a combination rook (horizontally and vertically) and bishop (diagonally) in any direction and over any distance of unoccupied squares.

Castling is the option that a player has of moving both a king and rook on the same move. This is done to safeguard the king and activate the rook. The king moves two spaces to the left or right, and the respective rook is placed on the adjacent square of the opposite side of the king. Castling is *the only move that allows two pieces to be moved on the same move.*

En passant captures occur when a pawn using its option of moving two spaces on its first move is captured by the opponent's pawn (situated on the 5th rank) as if the pawn had moved only one space.

Promotion or Queening occurs when a pawn reaches the 8th rank, whereupon it gets the option of promoting to queen, rook, bishop, or knight. This unique move is commonly called "queening" because the pawn generally promotes to a queen, the strongest piece.

The three special moves mentioned above – castling, pawn promotion and taking in passing (*en passant*) – are further expanded on in the following discussions.

The below Diagrams 1.7, 1.8, and 1.9 illustrate castling. The starred squares of Diag. 1.7 represent the squares on which the king will rest after it has executed castling to a respective side. The castling symbol is made with zeroes. If you had castle queenside, the chess notation would be **1. 0-0-0** for the three squares that the *rook* moved instead of two.

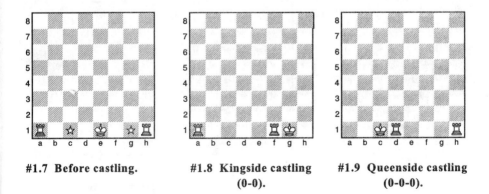

#1.7 Before castling.   #1.8 Kingside castling   #1.9 Queenside castling
                                    (0-0).   (0-0-0).

3

A couple of rules regarding castling are that (1) you cannot castle if the king or rook (on the side to which you are castling) has moved, and (2) you cannot castle *out of* or *through* check. If you are in check, you must first get out of check before you can castle. Not being able to *castle through check* is illustrated by Diag. 1.10.

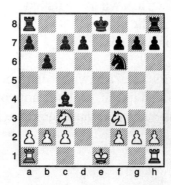

#1.10 White cannot castle to the kingside.

If you are able to get one of your pawns to the opponent's last rank (the eight row or – from White's view – a8 through h8; or correspondingly from Black's side, a1 through h1), then you can promote your pawn to any piece except another king or pawn. (You can have 9 queens of the same color on the board!) Diagrams 1.11 and 1.12 illustrate pawn promotion.

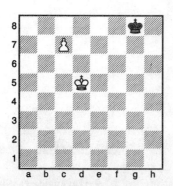

#1.11 Before promoting.

#1.12 After promoting to a queen: c8 = Q+.

The third special rule that we must learn is that of capturing a neighboring pawn when it attempts to pass one of your pawns. Taking in passing (or *en passant*) is possible if your pawn has reached the fifth rank and your opponent moves a neighboring pawn pass it by using its optional two moves. Then you have the option of capturing the pawn as if though it only moved one square. However, *you must take the pawn on your next move or else you lose the right to capture that particular pawn in passing.* Diagrams 1.13, 1.14, and 1.15 illustrate taking in passing (*en passant*).

#1.13 En passant staged.

#1.14 After f4 by White.

#1.15 En passant executed.

Over the centuries the rules of chess have evolved (particularly European chess) to grant the pieces more flexibility and power. The *en passant* capture was introduced into European chess between 1200 and 1600, soon after (1) castling was introduced, (2) the queens and bishops were given unlimited range along their trajectory, and – more pertinently – (3) pawns were granted the option of moving two squares on their first move. The *en passant* capture was introduced to prevent a pawn from using the novel two-square move to pass another pawn and thus evade capture. Some authorities state that the ruling was not universally accepted until the Italian rules were changed in 1880, but most agree that the rule was added during the 15th century. As for chess culture, the Asian chess variants do not recognize *en passant* captures because they were separated from the European chess development during that period.

The ABC's of Getting Out of Check

The object of chess is to checkmate your opponent's king. The king is checkmated when it is checked (attacked) and cannot get out of check. There are three methods that may be used to get out of check: abandoning the square that is under attack, blocking the attack of the checking piece, and capturing the attacker. These three methods we call *the ABC's of responding to checks* as a mnemonic to help you recall the options: **A**bandoning the attacked square, **B**locking the attacker, and **C**apturing the attacker. These three methods of escaping from check are illustrated below.

#1.16 White must Abandon the square by running to d2.

1.17 White must Block with g3.

1.18 White must Capture with Nxh4.

Keep in mind that you cannot block a knight's attack because his attack point is upon a square rather than along a file or diagonal.

Now for another history lesson! Chess as practiced in America and Europe is thought to have spread from Persia through the Moors into Spain. The terms of "chess" and "checkmate" originated in Persia. The Persian word for king was "shah." The word underwent several transformations and one of its variants became the Old French (e)schek. And (e)schek translates into the English term "check." Then this was simplified to Saxon and Modern English into "chess." The term "checkmate" is derived from the Persian "shah mat," which means "the king (shah) is dead (mat). Checkmate!

6

The Algebraic Chess Board

Setting up a chess game is easy if you follow this one simple rule:

White to the right and Queen on the color.

This simply means to set the board up so that a white square is located to your right-hand side. Then place the queen on the same color of the pieces that you conduct. (If you are keeping a score of the game and have a lettered board, the rightmost white square of the White pieces should be the h1-square.)

The below diagram illustrates the numbering system that is used for annotating a chess game. (The Descriptive Notation numbering system where each square has two names is included later in the *Advancing in Chess* feature of this section.) The ranks (from top to bottom, horizontal) are numbered from 1 to 8. The files (from left to right, vertical) are annotated from a through h. Therefore, in the diagram the black queen is located on **d8**. The White knight to the right of the White king is located on **g1**.

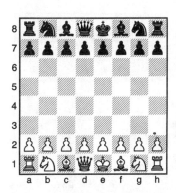

#1.19   Initial board setup.

Recording Moves

Because each square of the algebraic chess board has a unique name, recording moves is simple. If White moves the pawn in front of his king up two squares, his move is annotated as: **1. e2-e4**. If Black responds by playing his kingside knight up two squares and one toward his king, then his move is written as **1 ... Nf6**. (The ellipses signify that White's move has been already been made.)

His move could also have been described as **1 ... g8-f6** or **Ng8-f6**. Alternatively, White's first move could have been written as simply e4 since only that pawn could move to that square. Note that pawn moves do not have a capital "P" attached to them (1. Pe2-e4). The complete move pair could be written as: **1. e2-e4 Nf6**.

To be able understand chess notation and record your game is important for a number of reasons: (1) so that you can later study your game and avoid repeating the same mistakes; (2) so that you can make claims such as "draw by three-fold repetition" or "50-move rule"; (3) so that you can have a permanent memory of the game and get it printed; and (4) so that you can learn to read others' games and learn techniques from books. Now some additional sample moves will be presented and illustrated to help you learn chess notation.

1. **e2-e4**, Diag. 1.20. You can also use the shorthand version and simply record 1. e4. Black responds with 1... **d7-d5** (Diag. 1.21). White's second move is **d2-d4**, and Black responds with **2... N(b8)-c6** (Diag. 1.22). Note that the shorthand version has been used in the diagram to denote that the knight

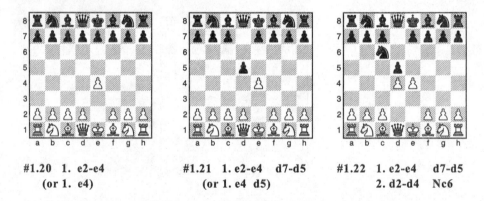

#1.20 1. e2-e4   #1.21 1. e2-e4   d7-d5   #1.22 1. e2-e4   d7-d5
     (or 1. e4)   (or 1. e4 d5)   2. d2-d4   Nc6

moves to the square c6. White answers this with a knight move of his own: **3. N(b1)-d2** (Diag. 1.23, next page). You can also say "3. Nb1-d2," but it looks a little cluttered. The shorthand notation would be "3. Nd2" or even just "3. Nd." Next, **3... e7-e5, 4. N(g1)-f3** (Diag. 1.24). Regarding the latter move, you had to say where the knight came from since either knight could have moved to f3.

8

#1.23	1. e2-e4	d7-d5		#1.24	1. e2-e4	d7-d5
	2. d2-d4	Nc6			2. d2-d4	Nc6
	3. N(b1)-d2				3. N-d2	e7-e5
					4. N(g1)-f3	

Black's fourth move is to take the e-pawn: **4... d5xe4** (Diag. 1.25). An "**x**" signifies captures or takes. White recaptures the pawn with the knight from d2. Note that in Diag. 1.25 either knight can capture a pawn. But even if one simply said "5. Nxe4" no reader would be confused (they would be, though, if you only said "5. Nxe). This is the main advantage of the long algebraic "from-to" notation: clarity. To this point, the complete game score sheet is:

. e2-e4 d7-d5; 2. d2-d4 Nc6; 3. Nd2 e7-e5; 4.N(g)-f3 d5xe4; 5.N(d2)xe4.

#1.25 4. ... d5 x e4

#1.26 5. Nd x e4

Earlier in this section (pps. 3 – 5) we mentioned that there are three special moves that the pawns and pieces have: castling, promoting, and capturing in passing (*en passant*). These special moves are notated as in the following diagrams. Partial diagrams have been used to show only the necessary portion of the chess board needed to illustrate the point.

The symbol for castling is made with zeroes. Castling is recorded by writing two zeroes for kingside castling (0-0) or three for queenside castling (0-0-0), representing the number of moves that the rook travels to park on the opposite side of the king. The "+" symbol signifies "check" and "++" indicates mate. (Just as you don't have to say "check" in a game, you don't have to write check!). Though you can be exact and write "**e.p.**" in Diagram 1.32 for capturing *en passant*, you aren't required to do so. (Note that Black can take the f-pawn if it moves two squares but cannot take the d-pawn which has already moved to d4.) You must capture in passing immediately or you forfeit your right to do so!

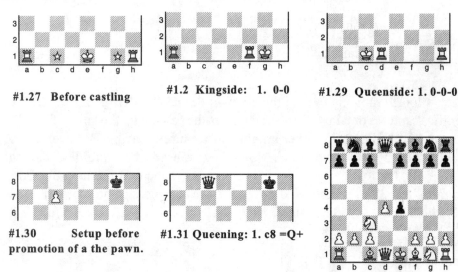

#1.27 Before castling

#1.2 Kingside: 1. 0-0

#1.29 Queenside: 1. 0-0-0

#1.30   Setup before
promotion of a the pawn.

#1.31 Queening: 1. c8 =Q+

#1.32 If a White 4. f4,
then 4... exf e.p.

The Alphabet of Responding to Attacks

Earlier in the *ABC's of Getting Out of Check*, three methods were given to get out of check: abandoning the square that is under attack, blocking the attack of the checking piece, and capturing the attacker. These are the only three methods that the king can employ to get out of check. However, when pieces other than the king are under attack, three additional methods of avoiding capture may be possible. For completeness, I'll refresh your memory with the earlier mentioned options while presenting the other three methods, dubbing the presentation the *alphabet of responding to attacks* because it is based upon a alphabetized mnemonic.

10

In general, you have six methods of responding to attacks upon your pieces (other than the king):

Response to Attacks
Abandoning the attacked square
Blocking the attacker
Capturing the attacker
Defending the piece
Enriching the tactics by counter attack
Failing to respond

The method *failing to respond* may not be as it bad as it superficially sounds – as long as you actually see that your piece is attacked. You may have a valid reason for not moving the piece, such as a sacrifice. Therefore, when your opponent seemingly fails to respond to your attack, consider that he might be baiting you to take the piece before you gobble it up!

An attack upon your piece by a pawn, the lowest-valued unit, reasonably allows you but four of the options because all the pieces are higher-valued than the pawn. Therefore it is not often that one defends a piece attacked by a pawn when the piece can simply abandon the square. Likewise, defense is generally not an option when any lower-valued piece attacks a higher-valued one because the exchange is generally favorable to the attacker. For example, who does not rush to move their queen when a rook attacks it or backs off their rook when a bishop threatens it? Of course there are always exceptions! And it is knowledge of when to take exception to the rule that distinguishes the better player. Diagrams 1.33 and 1.34 (next page) illustrate a couple of such exceptions. In Diag. 1.33 White is simply restoring material equality; in Diag. 1.34, White fears that moving the knight will allow a mating attack to ensue before he gets his pieces out. Hence he may seriously consider N(b)-d2.

Because the option of failing to respond to an attack is well understood, this option will not be illustrated. Too, if one truly does not respond to an attack, it is because one did not see it. We will illustrate some instances where the player appears to be failing to respond to an attack but has a very good reason

#1.33 After being caught in the Center Fork Trick, White Defends with Bd3 to restore equality.

#1.34 White reasons that it might be better to Defend or simply abandon the knight to get another piece out.

for seemingly ignoring his piece's plight. Most of these instances are cases of counter attack or enriching the tactics.

An overly popular choice of lower-ranked chess players is Enriching the tactics rather than simply moving or defending their piece. Unless you are competent at tactics, you should avoid counter attacking when a simple retreat is adequate for maintaining the balance. A common mistake is illustrated in Diag. 1.35. After **1. Nxe4   d6,** White should simply retreat his piece, abandoning the square. However, he gave a dubious check with **2. Bb5+** (Diag. 1.36) and ran

#1.35 White Enriches the tactics with the unnecessary check of Bb5+, expecting Black to block with a piece. But ...

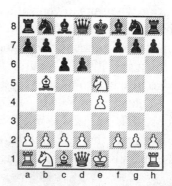

#1.36 Black Blocks the check with c6, obtaining an attack on two White pieces.

into the unexpected counter of **2... c6**. Feeling desperate, White further enriched the tactics with **3. Qh4?!**, hoping to sneak a mate in. However, **3... g6** embarrassed him even more (Diag. 1.37, below)!

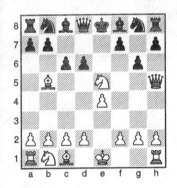

#1.37 White's continued aggression with Qh5 brings further sorrow after g6.

So that you won't get the incorrect impression that enriching the tactics is necessarily bad, consider the common case of Diag. 1.38 where White responds to a pawn push with the ideal of unleashing a crushing kingside attack if the h-file is allowed to be opened. Another related tactic is the kamikaze-piece. The piece simply captures another unit rather than passively waiting to be captured. In Diag. 1.39, White rightly figures that it is better to get the maximum compensation for the piece. Diagram 1.40 is a related example where White figures that it is better for him to enrich the tactics with **Bxf7+** rather than allow the pawn to take the bishop.

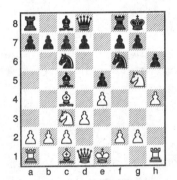

#1.38 The move 7. h4 is a common tactic where White seemingly Fails to respond but is actually Enriching the tactics.

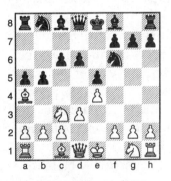

#1.39 White should play Nxb5!? gaining two pawns for the piece.

Consider all methods of responding to an attack before you select an option to deal with a threat to your pieces.

13

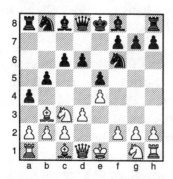

#1.40 Instead of allowing Black to ruin his pawn structure with axb, White prevents Black from castling with Bxf+, unleashing the kamikaze-piece.

The above statement is critical to good defense, a subject that is often overlooked during the lust to attack. *Knowing how to defend is just as important as knowing how to attack.* In fact, it is critical to stay defensive-minded even while engaged in attacking your opponent. To give you additional insight into defending, I have included some tips in the Appendix, *Conducting the Defense.*

Advancing in Chess: Descriptive Chess Notation

Before the system of Algebraic Chess Notation (or coordinate system) became popular, many countries used the Descriptive Notation. While it is not used much today, many older books and texts were written in it. Hence, to be able to get maximum benefit from reading a variety of chess books – many of which are too dated or voluminous to translate to the Algebraic system – it is important that you be able to understand both notation systems.

Though the Descriptive Notation is a mite cumbersome since each square has two names instead of only one as in the Algebraic system, it does have a logic that is easily understood. The notation refers to the initial position of the pieces, and the squares are numbered from the perspective of the side of the board on which you sit. That is, White's QR1 is Black's QR8. From White's viewpoint, pieces to the left of the queen are called "Queen's *whatever*" and pieces to the right of the king are called "King's *whatever*." The rooks at a1 and a8 are called Queen's Rooks; knights at b1 and b8 and called Queen's Knight; bishops at c1, c8 are called Queen's Bishops; bishops at f1 and f8 are called King's Bishops; knights at g1 and g8 and called King's Knights; and rooks at h1, and h8 are called King's Rooks. The pawns are designated by which piece they initially sit in front of: the pawn on b2 is called the Queen's Knight Pawn, and the pawn on f7 is called the King's Bishop pawn. See the figure below.

QR1	QN1	QB1	Q1	K1	KB1	KN1	KR1
QR8	QN8	QB8	Q8	K8	KB8	KN8	KR8
QR2	QN2	QB2	Q2	K2	KB2	KN2	KR2
QR7	QN7	QB7	Q7	K7	KB7	KN7	KR7
QR3	QN3	QB3	Q3	K3	KB3	KN3	KR3
QR6	QN6	QB6	Q6	K6	KB6	KN6	KR6
QR4	QN4	QB4	Q4	K4	KB4	KN4	KR4
QR5	QN5	QB5	Q5	K5	KB5	KN5	KR5
QR5	QN5	QB5	Q5	K5	KB5	KN5	KR5
QR4	QN4	QB4	Q4	K4	KB4	KN4	KR4
QR6	QN6	QB6	Q6	K6	KB6	KN6	KR6
QR3	QN3	QB3	Q3	K3	KB3	KN3	KR3
QR7	QN7	QB7	Q7	K7	KB7	KN7	KR7
QR2	QN2	QB2	Q2	K2	KB2	KN2	KR2
QR8	QN8	QB8	Q8	K8	KB8	KN8	KR8
QR1	QN1	QB1	Q1	K1	KB1	KN1	KR1

The Queen is abbreviated "Q"; King = K; Rook = R; Bishop = B; Knight = N or Kt; and Pawn = P. Castling and captures are designated the same as in the Algebraic system. Remember, Black's eighth row is White' first row; K4 (e5) to Black is White's K5. So White could play, say, 10. KN-K5 (f3-e5) and if Black captured with his knight at c6, then 10... QNxK4. You can also use short notation as in Algebraic notation: 10. N-K5 NxN (or Kt x Kt).

II. Opening Principles

Guidelines

Opening Principles
Control the center
Move only center pawns
Develop pieces
Castle early
Don't move the same piece before the other pieces have been developed – unless there is a forcing reason why you should do so
Don't bring out the queen too early

The reason that *Develop pieces* and *Castle early* are highlighted is in the hope that if you forget everything else you will still remember these two guiding principles while conducting your opening.

The main point that you concentrate on in the opening is developing your pieces. Get them off the back rank where they have no offensive impact. A piece still unmoved on the back rank is of no more active value than a piece which has been captured. When you do develop your pieces, choose good spots for them. A knight at f3 controls 8 squares while the same knight relocated to h3 controls only four. A bishop at h1 influences only 7 squares, but the same bishop placed at d5 controls 13 squares. Hence, centralize your pieces. Bring your pieces to bear on the center of the board. Here they have more impact: they are best placed for attack or defense. They observe both sides of the board and can quickly transfer to any other sector.

As a rule, the best place for the knight is at f3 (f6) and c3 (c6). (Note that if the opponent posts a knight early at f3 or f6 then there is no chance of getting in a Scholars' Mate!) The best spot for the bishop varies between f4 (f5) and c4 (c5) where they attack the center or g5 (g4) and b5 (b4) where they pin the opponent's knights, rendering them temporarily powerless. Make sure that the bishops are outside the pawn chain before you play d3 (d6) or e3 (e6),

17

depending upon whether you opened first with the king or queen pawn respectively. For the fastest castling opportunity, opening with e4 is preferred.

Only after castling and completing development should your start conducting an attack. At this stage, make sure that all of your pieces can quickly swing into action. If you are at lost as to what to do, **don't** push a pawn. See if you can safely post one of your pieces deeper into your opponent's territory; see if you can pin one of his pieces. **Try to improve the development of your worst-placed piece or the one which is doing less than the others.** Too, be cautious of snatching pawns before you have castled. Don't try to mate your opponent with the Queen early. With good defense, the attacker who tries these primitive tactics will generally either lose his queen early or seriously lag in development.

Remember, you can't fight a decent battle with half your army at home or if you are constantly tripping over your king. Get your pieces out and your king out of the way and into relative safety.

Ideal Opening

It is important to mobilize your pieces according to sound opening principles. While it is helpful to have book knowledge of an opening and its variations, you can play an acceptable game just by observing opening principles. After all, at the scholastic level, one-move mistakes predominate to such an extent that obtaining a slightly inferior opening has no actual impact on the ultimate outcome of the game.

Chief among the principles to be observed is the need to castle. Castling by itself will prolong most games by 10 moves. This is because the king has been removed from the center of the board and some pieces will have necessarily been developed. To achieve this objective, this lesson will lead you to a reasonable sequence of moves to activate your pieces.

Because playing e4 allows you to castle the sooner, we will concentrate on this as a first move. So White plays **1. e4**, establishing initial control over d5 and f5. See Diag. 2.1, next page. Note that this move also allows his king-bishop to develop. Although this move also frees his queen for movement, this is of less importance because you are better off not moving your queen out into the

 # 2.1

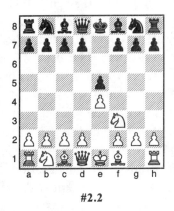

#2.2

fray during the early stages of the game. It will only get harassed by the pawns and pieces, helping your opponent to develop his forces with a gain of time. (We'll mention early queen moves later in the next section when we talk about the dreaded *Scholars' Mate.*) To obtain an equal share of the center, Black usually responds with **1 ... e5**.

Now White must make a decision on which piece to bring out. He can't be sure just where the Bishop might belong for it may be just as effectively posted at b5 as it would be at c4. He can be sure that the best square for the knight is f3, though. If you place the knight on h3 it can later be captured by the black bishop from c8, doubling your kingside pawns. If you place the knight at e2, it will block the bishop's development. Hence, **2. Nf3** is the preferred move (Diag. 2.2 positioning the knight where it controls some central squares (d4 and e5). Note, too, that the knight develops with a gain of time by attacking Black's e-pawn. Now Black should respond with a move that protects his e-pawn.

Let us digress briefly and state that many players actually do play 2. Bc4 first (Diag. 2.3) instead of 2. Nf3. This is often played at the scholastic level

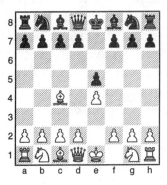

#2.3

because the player hopes to try to sneak in a quick mate with either Qh5 or Qf3 followed by Qxf mate. This is the notorious *Scholars' Mate.* If defended properly these moves should backfire on White because of the time lost moving his queen around. The best antidote to this scheme is to post the Black knight at f6. Then the queen can't go to h5 without being captured and the f7-square is shielded from the queen if it is placed at f3. (See *Scholars' Mate* in following section for more on this risky opening.)

Resuming our opening sequence, Black could play 2... d6. This move solidly protects the e-pawn and allows Black's queenside bishop to be developed. However, it locks in Black's kingside bishop. He could try 2... Bd6 but this keeps the d-pawn from advancing and halts the development of his queenside. Any queen moves by Black at this stage would be bad for they would halt the development of Black's other pieces or expose the queen. The best move for

#2.4

Black is **2... Nc6** because it: (1) develops a piece, (2) protects the pawn, and (3) controls the center. See Diag. 2.4, below.

Now White has only to develop one more piece before he can castle. Where should he place his bishop? Well, he could place his bishop at e2, but it starts looking like a pawn after d3 and 0-0. He could place it at d3, but then the other bishop's development suffers. The best move seems to be **3. Bc4**. From this post the bishop controls a center square and eyes Black's sensitive f7 square. Now Black needs to catch up in development before White actually does launch an attack. A good move for this purpose is **3... Bc5**

#2.5 After 3... Bc5.

(Diag. 2.5), copying White's move and avoiding the attack that White could start if Black played, instead, 3... Nf6. The potential consequences of 3... Nf6 will be treated later under the discussion of the Fried Liver Attack, page 28.

From Diagram 2.5, White is now in the position to castle or continue developing pieces. Either move is good. Let's continue with 4. Nc3, developing a piece and establishing further control over d5. Now both White and Black control a center square with three defenders.

Black again copies White's move and continues logically with 4... Nf6, developing a piece that attacks the center and makes room for castling. See Diagram 2.6 of the following page.

Both players control an equal share of the center; both players have only one other minor piece to develop; and both players can now castle.

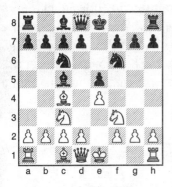

#2.6 After 4... Nf6.

Though 5. d3 would also be an excellent move at this stage, White can simply castle (**5. 0-0**), removing his king from the center of the board and bringing his rook toward the center where it can be more active. Black's best response is also to castle (**5... 0-0**), giving Diag. 2.7. Note that White has only one minor piece that is still on the back rank, his queenside bishop. To activate it, he plays **6. d3**, opening up the bishop's diagonal. See Diagram 2.8.

#2.7 After 5... 0-0.

#2.8 After 6. d3.

#2.9 After 6... d6.

Note that the pawn move also adds additional protection to his e4-pawn. This is important because it now means that his knight is no longer tied to the defense of the pawn. Hence the knight is now in the position to start thinking about attack, considering moves such as Na4 (attacking the bishop) or Nd5 (attacking the knight). Black needs to hurry and match White's development else he could be unprepared when the attack starts. Hence, he also should stabilize his center with a pawn and develop his other bishop. Therefore, best is **6... d6**, giving us Diagram 2.9 (above).

Look at Diag. 2.9. Both Black and White have conducted the opening in a model fashion, making a minimum of pawn moves to free their pieces and castle early. To complete development, all White needs to do is to develop his other bishop. Placing the bishop at e3 or g5 are both good choices. After **7.**

Be3, (Diag. 2.10) White actually hopes that Black will take the Bishop and open up the f-file for his rook to participate in a coming kingside attack. Too, if the bishop is taken, note how the pawn strengthens White's center with a black-square defender of d4 and f4. On the other hand, if White plays **7. Bg5** (Diag. 2.11), then he could well be planning on playing 8. Nd5 to double attack Black's pinned knight at f6 – later ripping the pawns apart and planning a kingside breach.

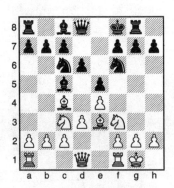

#2.10 After 7. Be3, White hopes that Black trades.

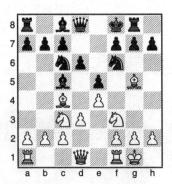

#2.11 After 7. Bg5, White plans Nd5, attacking the kingside.

Your placement of your bishop depends on which attack you like best. The main thing is to get it off the back rank and post it where it is doing something active. This not only activates the bishop but allows the rooks to cooperate with each other. Note that we did not move a single piece twice until the other pieces were developed. It is only after our pieces have been developed that we start thinking about attacking or winning something.

If you are wondering how to attack your opponent now that you have gotten your pieces out, then refer to *"Attacking from the Standard Position"* in the Appendix.

But what if Black responds with a move other than 1... e5? Well, there are six more common opening setups that we must be prepared to face. (The standard setup that we just detailed is called the Two [or Three] Knights Variation.) Though it is difficult to name an opening after only one move, the diagrams below have been given the name of the opening into which they most usually progress. The two or three moves that briefly describe the opening are given as suggestions on how the openings generally proceed. Be careful, though, because the openings can transpose into each other or into other strange, less common openings. But don't fear. All transpositions can be handled if you simply stick with good opening principles: (1) fight for control of the center, (2) move no more than two pawns before castling, (3) develop pieces, (4) castle early, and (5) don't attack too soon.

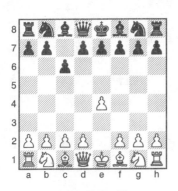

#2.12 Caro-Kann

1. e4	c6
2. d4	d5
3. Nc3	.

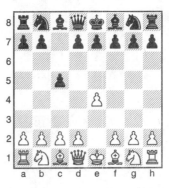

#2.13 Sicilian Defense

1. e4	c5
2. Nf3	d6
3. d4	cxd5

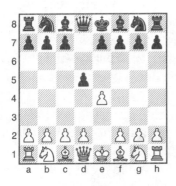

#2.14 Center Counter

1. e4	d5
2. exd	Qxd5
3. Nc3	

#2.15 French Defense

1. e4	e6
2. d4	d5
3. e5	

23

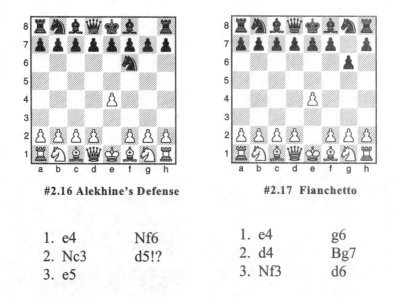

#2.16 Alekhine's Defense   #2.17 Fianchetto

1. e4	Nf6		1. e4	g6
2. Nc3	d5!?		2. d4	Bg7
3. e5			3. Nf3	d6

This brief treatment simply introduces the names of some common opening responses to 1. e4. And it is certainly not comprehensive because it neglects many other common openings, such as the Petroff Defense (1. e4 e5; 2. Nf3 Nf6). The suggested lines – such as given in Diagram 2.16 against the Alekhine's Defense – are not necessarily the best lines to obtain an advantage against the defense. (Most authorities strongly recommend 2. e5 instead of 2. Nc3.) This sketch of the e4-openings simply suggests easy methods of meeting the opening counters without getting bogged down in excessive theory.

If you want to develop any confidence playing against these openings, it is highly recommended that you learn more lines of the opening – at least 8 moves deep – or up to the point where you castle. With all the great opening chess books available, it is a waste of time for you to try to create an opening sequence from scratch during competition. Learn a little about the variations that you may be facing before the combat begins.

Scholars' Mate

This simple mate shamefully demands a section of its own because it rules at the scholastic level. It seems that everyone wants to try to catch new players is this ancient mate. However, the Scholars' Mate really is a wasteful attempt that brings the Queen out too early and retards the would-be mater's development if it is properly defended. This lesson will focus on how to prevent Scholars' Mate and to turn the tables on any who would attempt this against you.

First of all, let me emphasize that if you look one move ahead and ask questions like "What is attacked?" you will not fall for this easily defended mate. Now let us set up this simple mate from the start and show how to counter it.

The game opens **1. e4 e5** with both players correctly trying to control the center. Now White plays **2. Bc4**. This should signal to the alert player that White may be attempting the Scholars' Mate because it is known that the old adage of *"Knights before Bishops"* applies here. Remember, you know that the White knight belongs at f3. By not immediately placing it here, White signals that he might have other plans. Now let us make the same move for Black so

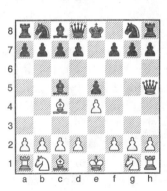

#2.18 Scholar's Mate at f7 set

that White can get in his superficial mating attempt: **2... Bc5**. Now White triumphantly plays **3. Qh5**. See the Diagram 2.18. Note that he simultaneously attacks e5 and f7. White is counting on Black overlooking his double attack. Again, if a player simply looks at everything that is attacked at each move, he could avoid loses due to inattention. However, many players see the e5 pawn under attack and automatically play 3... Nc6?? allowing 4. Qf7 mate. Equally bad, though, is trying to stop the mate on f7 by playing 3... g6. Now 4. Qxe5+ forks the king and the rook at h1. The best move to defend both pawns is 3... Qe7! Now Black can later play Nf6 and actually be ahead of White in development since White must retreat his queen for a lost of time. **When your opponent violates opening principles, you may need to do so also** to counter his aggression. Don't blindly adhere to the principles.

If Black simply plays 2... Nf6 on the second move in response to 2. Bc4, Scholars' Mate can't even be attempted. See Diag. 2.19. If White responds 3. Qh5?, then 3... NxQ wins. And he can't try to mate with 3. Qf3 because the knight on f6 blocks the attack on the f7 pawn. So **an early knight to f6 rules out the Scholars' Mate**. Once the queen is allowed to get to h5, though, it is too late to bring out the knight!

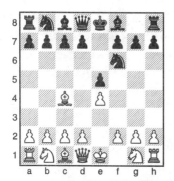

#2.19 Nf6 stops the attempt.

The Scholars' Mate is such a waste of time, though, that many good players encourage White to try it! They make a different second move that allows White to try the long form of the mate with a continued attack on f7. Let us look at how White can be encouraged to hang himself. On move 2, Black plays **Nc6**. See Diag. 2.20. Now White rushes in with **3. Qh5**. This is a different position, though! Note that our pawn at e5 has the knight defending it. This means that there is only a real attack on f7. Now the best way to defend this is to play **3... g6**, chasing the queen with a gain of time. What you should not play in this position is 3... Nh6?! See diagram 2.21. Remember, the king's knight belongs at f3 or f6, respectively. If you played like this, White could now try 4. d4. Now if 4... exd, then 5. Bxh, again leaving f7 unprotected (see Diagram 2.2, next page). So stick to 3... g6 in this position.

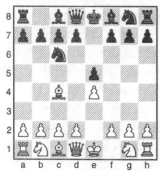

#2.20 Black entices White.

After 3... g6, if White plays **4. Q-f3**, again threatening mate (Diagram 2.23 of next page), Black has simply to look one move to see the cheap mate threat. He then plays the simple and best **4... Nf6**, blocking the mate and developing the knight to its best spot. Black has repealed the mating threat twice. But if White decides not to cautiously develop his queenside knight but rather to continue assaulting the f7-pawn, he can

#2.21 Black's defense lacks.

swing his queen to b3: **5. Qb3**. See the below Diag. 2.24. However, now **it is Black who has the winning game!**

#2.22 White removes the defender and threatens mate.

#2.23 After 3. Qh5 g6; 4. Qf3, White again threatens mate on f7.

#2.24 Black can ignore White's attack and start his own!

With **5... Nd4** Black attacks the White queen (see Diag. 2.25, below), daring White to take the pawn on f7 with check! For if he does, then there will be no white square available from which he can defend the bishop. And, therefore, he would simply lose the bishop.

After, 5... Nd4, White must protect the vulnerable c2-pawn and the e4-pawn. Therefore he plays **6. Qd3.** Now Black can assume a winning attack with **6... d5!** (Diagram 2.26), basing his pawn sacrifice on the idea that any capture of the pawn allows Bf5, attacking the queen and the c2-pawn. Learn these winning variations yourself and then play them on some would-be mater!

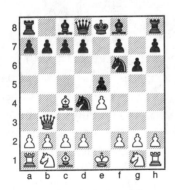

#2.25 White is in trouble.

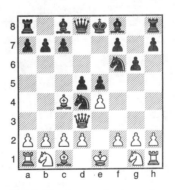

#2.26 Black sacs for more!

27

Though this approach to the Scholar's Mate is viable and preferable, I have found that rank beginners still end up losing material or getting checkmated when confronted with the attack. Hence after another decade of coaching since the first edition of this book was published, I recently devised an even simpler approach that has proven to be more easily grasped and usable by beginners (especially those still in kindergarten).

You advise them to try to copy White's moves. If White moves a bishop, they should develop a bishop. If he moves a knight, they should move a knight. Though Black may not be playing the most spirited chess, this simplified approach may help the inexperienced escape being quickly mated.

Now let's see how this works in practice. As detailed earlier on page 19, Black counters White's **1. e4** with **1... e5** maintaining equal control of the center. Now if White continues **2. Bc4**, Black should develop his bishop, also: **2... Bc5**. This yields Diagram 2.27, below.

If White continues with **3. Qh5** (Diag. 2.28), then note that he attacks three points: h7, f7, and e5. And only h7 is properly defended. See the below diagram. Both f7 and e5 need defense, and only a queen move by Black can defend both points simultaneously. The preferable queen move is to e7, leaving f6 available for the Black knight's development. Though Black could have replied 3... Qf6 to defend his pawns and simultaneously launch an attack on White's f2-square, this would be unnecessarily aggressive at this point. Hence, **3... Qe7** is recommended, producing Diagram 2.29.

#2.27 Black answers 2. Bc4 with 2... Bc5.

#2.28 White attacks three points and threatens the Scholar's Mate on f7.

#2.29. White's queen move is canceled by Black's queen move.

If White next develops a knight, so will Black. The justification for Black's early queen move is quickly seen if White continues **4. Nc3**. For – seeing nothing immediately attacked – Black strikes back with **4... Nf6**, hitting White's queen. See Diagram 2.30. Now if the White queen slinks back to d1, Black can simply play Q-d8, himself, and it is as though the queens never moved. (Of course, Black can also continue development with Nc6 and remain a tempo up.)

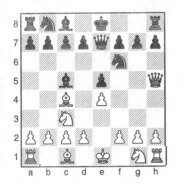

#2.30. Black gains a tempo off White's queen, which fully justifies his earlier queen move.

If White continues aggressively from Diagram 2.29, previous page) and plays **4. Nf3**. We get Diag. 2.31 below. Black should pause and ask "What's attacked?" Then upon seeing that his pawn on e5 is being attacked again, he counters with a knight move of his own, developing his queenside knight to defend the pawn on e5: **4... Nc6**. This yields Diag. 2.32. If White continues with 5. Nc3 or 5. 0-0, Black develops with 5... Nf6, hitting the queen. But if White continues aggressively with **5. Ng5!?** (Diag. 2.33), Black needs only to ask "What's attacked?" to find the best move.

#2.31 White continues the attack with 4. Nf3 (instead of playing 4. Nc3).

#2.32 After 4. Nf3 (attacking e5), Black develops his knight to defend the pawn.

#2.33 After 5.Ng5!? – again hitting f7 – Black needs additional defense.

Examining Diag. 2.33, you will notice that both h7 and f7 have been attacked again. Though it may seem convenient to answer the White knight's move with a knight move of your own (Nh6), this is an excellent time to stop copying White's piece moves. So – rather than awkwardly placing your knight at h6 – it is even stronger for Black to launch his own attack now with **5... g6!** This gives us Diag. 2.34, below. Now White gets into difficulties for he must keep his knight defended. If he plays 6. Qg4? then 6... d5 wins a piece. And after **6. Qh4**, then **6... h6!** is strong, threatening Qxg5, Diag. 2.35. Now it does not

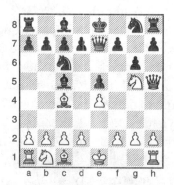

#2.34 More effective to repel White's attack is 5. ... g6!

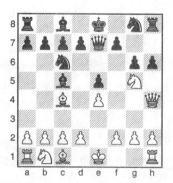

#2.35 After 6. Qh4 h6!, Black's counter-attack assures him an advantage.

matter that White can continue with 7. Bxf7+ Kg8, 8. Bxg8 Kxg8 because after Black later plays Nd4 – taking advantage of White's undeveloped pieces and attacking c2 – Black will have a slight advantage. So – as usual for premature attacks – White's aggression rebounds on him later if Black defends properly.

White does have two other attempts at the Scholar's Mate. If he plays 2. Qh5 before developing his bishop to c4, Black should notice that both f7 and e5 are under attack and counter by immediately moving his queen to e7, yielding Diag. 2.36 of the next page. However if White instead plays 2. Qf3, Black should see that only f7 is attacked and play the very strong 2... Nf6, developing a piece and shielding the f7-square. Note how out of place the queen appears to be in Diag. 2.37 (see following diagram).

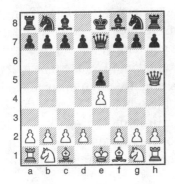

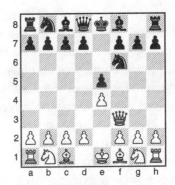

#2.36 Black copies White.   #2.37 Black develops logically.

Though the early queen move by Black seems to violate usual recommendations, it is justified because White himself has deviated from proper opening principles. And, as has been shown, Black can get a good game by copying White's moves.

So you now have the tools to handle the Scholars' Mate. But don't get caught by me or your coach playing it in competition! It was near detestable for me to dignify Scholars' Mate by this presentation. However, my intent was to show that it is not to be feared and will often boomerang on the perpetrator. I want to demystify it to the beginner and to expose it as a fraud, a lazy person's attempt to capitalize on an opponent's lack of experience without expending any imagination of their own.

Summarizing, after 2. Bc4, you can simply prevent Scholars' Mate by playing 2... Nf6 or you can encourage it by playing 2... Nc6. Further, if you are instructing those with poor tactical abilities and little experience, then the "copying" approach with the idea of matching piece moves may be preferable. All of these approaches give you a very good game. The Scholars' Mate is simple to defend if handled correctly – but it has killed many a beginning player and will continue to do so.

Advancing in Chess: Aggressive Opening Play

Recall that when you were first taught how to open a chess game, there was strong focus on observance of the opening principles emphasized in this section. Your teacher wanted to assure that you simply got out of the opening with a fair game. There was no consideration given to White trying to obtain an opening advantage – or even avoiding a slightly inferior opening. This is because one-move blunders predominate at the scholastic level. Now that you have progressed, you do need to try to be a little more exact in the opening because you are a better player and your opponents are tougher. Hence it is time that we put a little spice into your opening so that you can garner some quick kills and keep your opponents off balance.

First of all, if you decide to use some of these opening tactics, then you should read an opening book or research your particular variation in an online database before you venture to play it. Then you should find games played with your opening variation by stronger players and study them. Next you should test your new knowledge of the opening in over-the-board play or against the computer.

We will focus on one particular variation that comes from the Two Knights Defense (Italian Variation 4. Nc3 [ECO code C55]) or the Four Knights Defense. Since 1. e4 is typically played, we'll look at sharpening Black's 1... e5 with an eye to snatching an early advantage and upsetting White who perhaps just wants to get out of the opening safely. Our starting position comes after **1. e4 e5; 2. Nf3 Nc6; 3. Bc4 Nf6**. See Diag. 2.38.

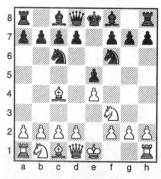

#2.38 An early crisis point.

Now many players have been taught to develop their pieces in the opening so they rush to play 4. Nc3 to protect their e-pawn. Well, this is the basis for a little trap if Black immediately attacks White's center. For example, **4. Nc3 Nxe!; 5. Nxe d5**. See Diag. 2.39 on the following page. Now the best moves for both sides are **6.Bd3 dxe4; 7.Bxe4 Bd6; 8.d4 ...** (**8.Bxc6+ bxc6 9.d4 e4!** Black stands better because of his two bishops and control of the open files.) **8... exd4** (better than 8...Nxd4; 9.Nxd4 exd4; 10.Qxd4 Qe7);

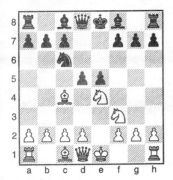

#2.39 White has been caught by the Fork Trick.

9.Bxc6+ bxc6; 10.Qxd4 (10.Nxd4 0-0 ll.Nxc6 Qh4); 10 0-0; 11.0-0 c5; 12.Qc3 Bb7. On this concluding position, Grandmaster Ludek Pachman states in The *Opening Game in Chess* (1986): "With a good position for Black. Despite his weakened pawn structure his two bishops give him a strategical advantage."

Well, suppose White is not so compliant and – after 4... Nxe! (refer to Diag. 2.40 below) – plays 5. Bxf+ instead of an immediate 5. Nxe? Things actually appear worse for White than in our first variation! Let's see . **After 5. Bxf+ Kxf; 6. Nxe d5; 7. N(e)-g5+ Kg8** (see Diag. 2.41); **8. d3** (to protect the knight at g5 against the threat of e4, chasing away its defender) **h6; 9. Nh3 Bxh; 10. gxh** and Black is the equivalent of a pawn up. Black will simply "castle by hand" later, with Kh7 and rook either to e8 or f8.

#2.40 What if White checks on f7 before capturing the knight?

#2.41 Though aggressively placed, it is White who is in trouble.

For those of you who are troubled that their favorite opening seems to have a slight flaw, don't panic. You can simply play 4. d3 instead of 4. Nc3. Then after some normal Black move, you can play your knight to c3, arriving at your comfortable position. (See *Ideal Opening*, page 21.) However, Black does not have to be so cooperative! After 4.d3, Black can attack the center with 4... d5!? See Diag. 2.42, next page. Though Black actually has a slightly worse evaluation than if he just allowed White to simply transpose into the Guioco

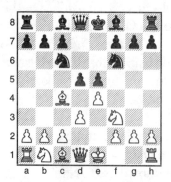

#2.42 After 4. d3, Black can attempt to seize the initiative.

Piano, the move could be worth playing just to get White out of his comfort zone. No worry – we have even better stuff planned for White! Keep reading!

Here is another enterprising try for Black to use against relatively-inexperienced opponents. Though these openings can be used to win against stronger opponents, they aren't recommended because against a good defender you might have to work a little harder than usual to reorganize your position. Still, these system might be worth trying just for the surprise value!

After the standard opening of **1. e4 e5; 2. Nf3 Nc6; 3. Bc4**, White is hoping for the tame 3... Nf6 or 3... Bc5. However, Black throws in an aggressive counter that must be handled carefully: 3... Nd4?! See Diag. 2.43. Now if White plays 4. Nxe, he is the one losing after 4... Qg5! (Diag. 2.44).

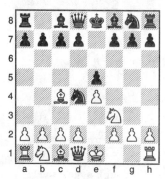

#2.43 Black plays 3... Nd4!?

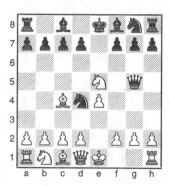

#2.44 Black wins in all lines.

Now if 5. Bxf+ Ke7; 6. Bxg Qxg; 7. Rf1 Qxe+; 8. Qe2 Qxe mate. Similarly, 5. Nxf Qxg; 6. Rf1 Qxe+; 7. Be2 Nf3 smothered mate. And this quick mate deserves a diagram: see Diag. 2.45, next page. About the best that White seems to be able to do (from the position of Diag. 2.44) is 5. Bxf+ Ke7; 6. Bd5 (to protect the sensitive e4-pawn) Qxg; 7. Rf d6 (driving off the defender of f3 and freeing the c8 bishop); 8. Nc4 Nf3!; 9. Ke2 Nxh; 10. Ne3 Qxf+!; 11. Nxf Bg4+ and Black is well ahead in material.

34

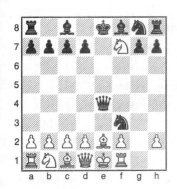

#2.45 A smothered mate.

If a good player is eager to give you a pawn in the opening, then think long before you capture it. After 3 ... Nd4?! (Diag. 2.43, previous page), White's best move is to simply castle (though c3 is also a good choice, playing to establish a broad center). Note that he will then have three pieces developed (knight, bishop, and castled rook) to Black's one piece, a badly placed knight.

Therefore, Black's best bet is to try to bail out and equalize the position by reducing White's power. Hence, 4. 0-0! Nxf+; 5. Qxf Qf6 (hoping to swap queens so that White's lead in development won't be so meaningful); 6. Qg3 Bc5 (to prevent an early f4 by White, exposing the Black queen to attack and f7) 7. Nc3 c6 and after d6 Black has reasonable changes of catching up in development.

Now we get to some excitement for White: an invitation to the Fried Liver Attack! If 3... Nf6, then if instead of protecting the e-pawn with Nc3 (allowing the Fork Trick, page 32) or d3 (allowing Black to attack the center, page 33), Ng5 sets up a promising attack position for White against the sensitive f7-pawn. After **1. e4 e5; 2. Nf3 Nc6; 3. Bc4 Nf6; 4. Ng5**, Diag. 2.46 results.

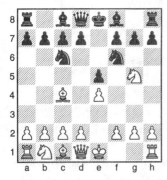

#2.46 White tries for the Fried Liver Attack.

The only way that the f7-pawn can be defended is to play 4... d5. Then there are two variations, one in which White remains a clear pawn up but has to suffer a tricky counter attack by Black and the other where White gets in the Fried Liver attack (giving up a piece for a few pawns and enduring initiative).   Let's take a look at this two variations.

After **4. Ng5 d5; 5. exd Na5** we get Diag. 2.47, next page. Now **6. Bb5+ c6; 7. dxc bxc; 8. Qf3 Rb8; 9. Bd3** (refusing to capture another pawn which would grant Black a significant lead in development and a vicious counter attack) **h6; 10. Ne4.** White lags in development and may have to suffer a tough attack. But he is a solid pawn up! Don't fret, though. Black has

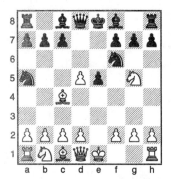

#2.47 Black sacs a pawn for quick development.

to know the analysis to play so strongly. This is why you are playing this variation against lesser opposition: even if you have a small negative your superior ability and experience with the opening should allow you to overcome – and you do have an extra pawn for the moment.

Now let us get to the variation that is more fun for White, the notorious Fried Liver Attack. If instead of 4... Na5 as above, 4... Nxd enters a web of complications (Diag. 2.48). Let us look at the main line of play. **4. Ng5 d5; 5. exd Nxd; 6. Nxf7 Kxf; 7. Qf3+ Ke6** (forced to defend the knight); **8. Nc3 N(c)b4**. See Diag. 2.49. At this point, White has three proven continuations: Qe4, 0-0, and even a3. The effectiveness of simply castling

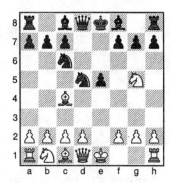

#2.48 White enters the Fried Liver Attack with 6. Nxf7.

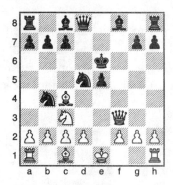

#2.49 White has three choices.

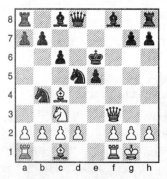

#2.50 White plays d4 or Qe4.

is a relatively recent discovery that was aided by the deep analysis that computers provide. Those variations rely on Black's greed to get him into further troubles. And, though a3 immediately gets a return of material, White forsakes castling. Hence I won't recommend this variation for scholastic players. So, **9. Qe4** (to defend c2 and pin the e-pawn) **c6** (to add more defense to d5 as a3 was threatened, driving a defender away); **10. a3 Na6; 11. d4 Nac7** (if 11... Kd7 12. Nxd5 is even better for White); **12. f4**. The position is probably only equal but Black is still going to have to survive the middle game and White is certainly not reluctant to enter an endgame since his pawns may be worth more than the piece. My preference for an advantage, though, is 9. 0-0. After 9... c6, White can still transpose with 10. Qe4 but I prefer the enterprising 10. d4 hoping that Black will try win the a1-rook. If White is able to timely get his rook to d1, he will have a won game.

Don't worry that you did not emerge with a huge advantage from playing the Fried Liver Attack. What I have shown is best play by Black. It is highly likely that Black will slip up and allow you a crushing attack. Too, unless your opponent has extensively studied this and the other openings that are in this section, you have a big advantage in that you are familiar with the variations. Hence you will recognize any deviations and know to look for refutations!

Advancing in Chess: Recommendations for Self-study

Books on Openings

To play good chess consistently, you will have to learn the nuances of an opening that suits your disposition and style. (You'll learn what your style is by playing more chess games or emulating those players whose games you enjoy going over. If you want instruction on how to identify your chess style or pinpoint what stage of your game needs more work, read *Chess for Tigers* by Simon Webb, Pergamon Chess.) In choosing an opening, it is important that you understand its variations, the ideas behind it, and are comfortable playing it. Once you have made this choice, seek to (1) find books by masters that reveal some finer points of the opening that you might be overlooking, (2) play different variations of the opening against your computer or test it with competition on the Internet, (3) keep abreast of the latest games utilizing the opening (you can download many games in portable game notation (pgn) format from the Internet or play through the latest games for free on many online chess sites), and (4) above all – don't abandon the opening just because you lose a few games with it!

However, if you consistently lose with your opening, have a stronger player analysis your games with you and advise you whether it is the opening or your subsequent weak play that is causing your loses. You can also use the analysis mode of some computer programs (ChessMaster or Fritz, for instance) to help you with this analysis. On the other hand, if playing a particular opening gives you a sense of power, adventure, or enthusiasm, don't be afraid to assay it no matter how many times you are thrashed! Just don't lose by the same blunder twice. As long as you are growing with the opening, you are progressing.

Too, don't take the *books'* recommendation as gospel. If you don't understand a particular variation, it does not matter that Kasparov and other grandmasters have a 90% winning record with it. You have to be comfortable with it. Play what you know and what suits you. Remember, the opening is a platform for getting your pieces developed in accord with the type of game that you wish to play. Master opening principles rather than memorize opening variations.

Just playing by opening principles can get one a long way in chess. For instance, I played a queen-pawn opening variation (the London System for White) for five years before I even knew that it was a recognized book line with a name! (I am not an zealous about opening theory.) I did well with the opening simply because it suited my style and the ideas were simple enough that well-booked opponents could not surprise me. If someone sprung something on me in the opening that was unfamiliar to me, I would simply analyze the threats and generate my response on the spot. This supports the argument that if you can understand the ideas behind your opening and can calculate well, then you don't have to know the latest theory to play acceptably at the amateur level. You simply write your own book with experience through over-the-board practice! Beware, though – you'll lose valuable clock time unless you know the opening to a sufficient depth (say, 10 moves deep).

Use the recommendations below to get you started in the opening and provide a foundation to specializing in the opening of your choice. Once you get a decent grounding, then go on to buy the specialized texts that deal with your opening in detail. Many of the books that I will recommend throughout this book are my choices simply because I have studied them and know that they are excellent. There are many other new books on the market that may have somewhat similar quality. Nonetheless, my picks have stood the test of time and chess players' scrutiny:

How to Play the Opening in Chess, Znosko-Borovsky, E.A., Dover, 1971. The book is in descriptive chess notation and is dated. However, it does present a very logical approach to learning chess openings, presenting the ideas behind the openings and common traps. It is a good introduction to openings for anyone who is below Class B (USCF 1800), and it lays a foundation for understanding the purpose of the opening and how it should be conducted.

The Ideas Behind the Chess Openings (Algebraic edition), Reuben Fine, Batsford, 1989. Again, the specific information is dated for those sharks among us who aspire to mastery. However, the explanation and content help prepare a player to learn an opening and get better with their choice of opening. If you supplement this book with the modern assessment of the particular line that you wish to play, you have an excellent foundation for both understanding and successfully using your opening.

Batsford Chess Openings 2 (also known as *BCO2*), Kasparov, G. and Keene, R., MacMillan Publishing Co., New York, 1989; or *Modern Chess Openings*, 15th edition (also known as *MCO-15*) by Nick Defirmian, David Mckay Co., New York, 2008 are one-volume opening encyclopedias. Both contain all the major lines and most popular lines of all openings (b3, c4, d4, e4, Nf3, g3, etc.). Because they present so much material, detailed analyses of a particular line may be lacking. However, the books offer a broad look at most openings that you will encounter. One of these books should be part of your reference library.

Chess Openings for Black, Explained by GM Lev Alburt, GM Roman Dzindzichashvili, and GM Eugene Perelshteyn (Chess Information and Research Center) 2nd edition. Copyrighted in 2009, this book provides a complete repertoire for Black against all reasonable White moves. The book talks about the ideas behind the openings and emphasizes grasping the flow of the opening rather than just memorizing lines. A companion volume, *Chess Openings for White, Explained* by the same authors give the same detailed treatment while recommending 1. e4. Incidentally, the authors recommend spending no more than 25% of your time studying openings.

Computer/Online Resources

There are excellent opening books published monthly. But with the popularity of the internet, it is no longer necessary to have the latest book at your finger tips because you can simply download the latest games from the internet and even explore entire openings using interactive databases. And, thankfully, many of these internet resources are free.

For instance, the free *Chess Tempo* website (chesstempo.com) features a chess opening database that you can search by opening name or moves. Moreover, this database is tied to their free online database of over two million games. So you can research your openings and instantly see how the top players fare when they use different variations of them in actual games. **Chess.com** also allows you to explore the openings by searches conducted by (1) player, (2) opening name, or (3) opening code. Moreover, you can instantly pull hundreds of games of your specific opening up for immediate play on a chessboard.

And speaking of online databases, you'll certainly want to check out *Chessbase's* database (www.chesslive.de) of over five million games that is updated daily with current play from important tournaments. This database is again being freely provided, though its free access was temporarily limited to those who purchase their suite of chess software (Chessbase, Fritz, Rybka, etc.). The popular **Chessmaster** software also provides a valuable survey of the openings that can be used to supplement books and improve your game.

Besides giving you instant access to a source of opening knowledge (you can access these by cellphone or laptop computer), these database resources give you more than games. They present statistics of how various branches from the main stem game evaluate as well as the average rating of the players who employ specific lines. Such tools as these reduce the need for current opening books because you can do your own research and comparison. However, until you are able to conduct your own reviews and make effective judgements about various lines, most beginners may benefit more from reading books.

It is no denying, though, that you can get the feel of an opening quicker by playing through many high quality games. By doing this you see how the opening transitions to the middle game. Hence you can judge whether an opening is more suitable to your style of play. With the internet or a chess database, you can download or review entire games in the time that it would take you to physically reset a chess board. These are valuable resources and should be used to broaden your grasp and knowledge of the opening.

III. Necessary Checkmating Skills

One of the most frequently-asked questions at scholastic tournaments where there are beginners is *"Is this mate?"* I've witnessed countless games where one player has an overwhelming material edge but can't mate the opponent's lone king. Therefore it behooves players to learn some mating techniques before they deal with any other topics. **COACHES:** It is best that you control your students' natural impulse to immediately plunge into a game until you are sure that they have at least one mating technique at their disposal – otherwise the game could go on almost forever!

Rook and King Mate

Because the rook gets less involved than the other pieces, it usually survives to the endgame. Hence the majority of mates are conducted with rooks (unless the player queens). So we will look at mating with the rook and king first, achieving a mate setup as illustrated in Diag. 3.1.

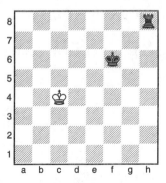

#3.1 King-rook mate.

#3.2 White has 40 squares.

Before the King can be mated, its available moves must first be restricted. (Refresh your memory of the options available to a King to avoid mate by referring back to *The ABCs of Getting Out of Check*, page 6.) It must be cornered or denied escape squares. One of the most useful techniques to know is that of **boxing in the King**: on each move decrease the number of squares available to it until you have it in a basic mating position. Some also refer to systematically decreasing the number of squares available for a King to move – or escape – as "fencing." You build ever-decreasing fences about the King, cutting down its range until you corral him and deliver a mate similar to Diag. 3.1.

In Diag. 3.2, **Black to move**, White has almost the whole board on which to roam. To mate

41

White, Black must systematically decrease its escape squares. White can now move to six squares, but there are 40 of the 64 squares on the Board that he can legally be on. We want to cut White's available moves down to only one or two. When we achieve this, then mate will follow shortly!

Black immediately cuts the potential squares that White can occupy in half (to 21) by playing **1... Rd8!**. Let's have White be stubborn by not helping us out by going to b3 or c3 when with 2...Rd5 we could cut his potential squares to only 12. White plays **2. Kc5,** approaching the Rook and trying to stay in the center. Black now brings his King over to help box the White King. **2... Ke6. 3. Kc6** (if King to the b-file, 3... Rc8!) **Rd5!,** decreasing the King's box to only nine moves, anyway! **4. Kb6 Kd6** (the box is getting smaller). **5. Kb7 Rc5!,** not letting the King escape to the f-file [note that 5... Rb5!! sets up a two-move mate or decreases the box to three squares]. **6. Kb6** (attacking the rook) **Kd5** (not letting the King out of the small box. **7. Kb7 Rc6** (four squares only!); **8. Kb8 Kd6; 9. Ka7 Kc7** (now only one square is available); **10. Ka8 Ra6 mate**.

The main principles of boxing can be summarized as:

1.   Use the Rook to initially take as many squares as possible from the White King.
2.   Use the Black King to assist the Rook and also capture squares.
3.   If the White King attacks the Rook, do not move it away allowing the White King to increase his freedom. Use the Black King to protect it and help limit White. (Remember: the King is a fighting piece in the endgame!)
4.   As the box decreases to four or less squares, be vigilant not to stalemate.
5.   Restrict the White King to a box of only two possible squares and look for a mate (similar to Diag. 3.1)!

If you can understand the basic mating pattern of the first diagram on the following page, then you have the tools to understand a whole family of mates. This mate theme is the most basic: the opposing King is boxed-in and checkmated. The restriction can be caused by friendly or enemy pieces; the effect is the same. In Diag. 3.3, below, note how Black's own pawns simply rob his king of an escape square. In Diag. 3.4, note how similar it is to the previous diagram after White plays Re1 mate. And the third of the diagrams below illustrates that the effect is the same whether it is your pieces or the opponent's pieces limiting the king's escape.

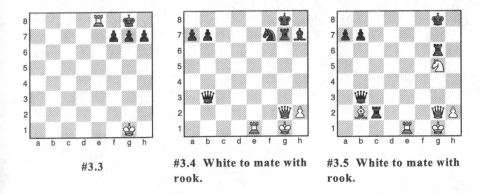

#3.3

#3.4 White to mate with rook.

#3.5 White to mate with rook.

Simple Queen-Assisted Mates

The queen-king mate is almost as common as the rook-king mate in top-level chess. In scholastic chess, though, there is generally ample opportunity to execute the queen-rook mate but the players generally run to get additional material before trying to deliver mate. So it is important to look at how mate is accomplished with these stronger forces.

The Queen-Rook mate one of the easiest mates to remember. The first of these three essential Queen-Rook mates is called the a step mate because the queen and rook methodically step across the board, checking the king and taking an entire file away at each move. Diagrams 3.6 – 11 of the following page illustrate this mate. The Triangle-Mate (or Rolling Check) is shown in Diagrams 3.12 – 17, where the queen and rook swing across the board supporting each other while giving check. (Note the triangle in Diagram 3.13 formed by the squares b3-d5-d3.) And finally, the more common Queen-King mate is shown is Diagrams 3.18-23. If you remember the last mate, it will save you a lot of time constructing a mate and help you avoid stalemating with the queen. You simply pin the opponent's king to the last rank and then don't check the king again until the mate is set.

43

Step Mate

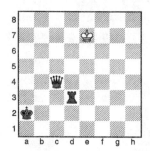

#3.6 By successive checks, Black to mate in 5 moves.

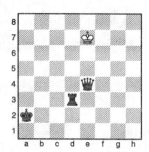

#3.7 Black forces White to the f-file.

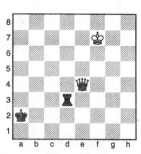

#3.8 Now Black is set to take the f-file with check.

#3.9 White is next driven to the g-file.

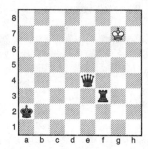

#3.10 White is next driven to the h-file with Qg4+.

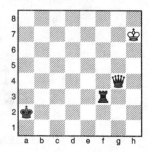

#3.11 The rook is set to mate with R-h3++.

Triangle Mate

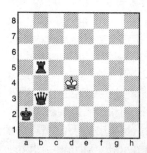

#3.12 Black to mate in 5 by alternating checks of rook and queen.

#3.13 First, the rook checks, pushing the king towards the edge of the board.

#3.14 Now the queen swings in with check, protected by the rook.

44

#3.15 The sequence of checks is repeated.

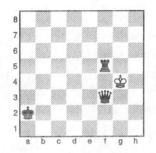

#3.16 The queen continues driving the king.

#3.17 And the sequence mate ends with a rook check.

King-queen Mate

#3.18 Black to avoid stalemating White and mate in 5 moves.

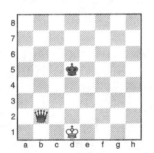

#3.19 The queen move is key, confining the White king.

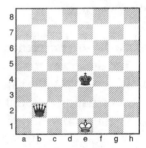

#3.20 Next, the Black king is brought closer.

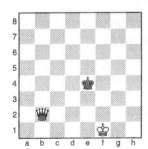

#3.21 White's moves are futile.

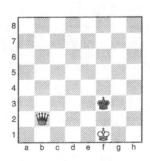

#3.22 The Black king approaches decisively.

#3.23 Only now does the queen move to finish.

Drawn Games

Games that are not decisive are drawn, producing a tie. There are five different ways in which a game can result in a draw. The last three of these draws exist as means of avoiding chess games that continue on endlessly without result.

(1) Draw by stalemate occurs when a player is unable to complete his turn because he lacks a legal move to play. Since his king is not directly attacked and he can't move it into check, the game is a draw. Because stalemate occurs so much and robs players of their generally huge material advantage – not to mention a half point! – we give this additional treatment on the next page.

(2) Draw by agreement can be reached by a draw offer of the player on the move being accepted by the other player. The player to whom the draw was offered can consider accepting the draw for as long as he wishes and until he makes a move on the board. If the opponent refuses the draw offer, then play simply continues.

(3) Draw by insufficient material occurs when neither player has enough pieces on the board to *force* a checkmate. Such a game could continue indefinitely with players shuffling pieces but having no means of getting a win. Insufficient mating material would be: (1) king vs. king, (2) king and knight vs. king, (3) king and bishop vs. king, (4) king and two knights vs. king, and (5) king and bishop vs. king and bishop of same color as opponent's bishop. If a player has at least one pawn remaining, then he has sufficient mating material because he has the possibility of queening.

(4) Draw by repetition of position occurs when the exact position appears on the board three different times at any point in the game with (1) all pieces and pawns located on the same squares, (2) the same player about to move, and (3) the pieces having the same options, such as the ability to castle. *The three identical positions need not occur on successive moves.* Moreover, there is technically no "repetition of moves" or "perpetual check" draw (because it is irrelevant that the draw claimant is delivering check). Examples of these occurrences are presented later in this section.

(5) Draw by the 50-move rule occurs when the player on the move claims a draw and demonstrates that 50 consecutive moves have been made by each side without any capture or pawn move. The fifty-move rule exists for the purpose of ending a game in which a player has failed to make progress towards administering checkmate in a timely manner. In some extremely rare endgame positions (i.e., queen vs. two knights) where the winning technique requires – even with best play – more than 50 moves to complete, a higher move limit (e.g. 75 moves) can be declared if such details are posted at the tournament before the start of the first round of play.

There is another important amendment to this rule of which players should be aware. If you are playing in a sudden death tournament (where the final or only time control requires that all moves be made in a specified time), *have less than 5 minutes remaining* on your clock, and have a simplified position where pawn captures are unlikely, you may request that the TD assist you in counting your moves. If the TD decides to honor your request, then you can be credited with moves already made toward achieving the 50-move draw. If you are playing in a scholastic tournament and have not been keeping score but wish to claim a draw by the 50-move rule, you can ask the TD to allow you to make a mark on a piece of paper for every move that the opponent completes. Because you had not been keeping score, the TD can use his discretion before granting you this privilege.

Now let us take a more detailed look at these important drawing situations.

Stalemate

Because stalemate is so pervasive (and perversive), we'll look at this event first. Moreover, it is very important that players be able to immediately distinguish

#3.24 **Black to move – stalemate!**

between checkmate (a win) and stalemate (a draw). Remember, for it to be checkmate, the king must be in check.

Let us take a look at a couple of diagrams so that we can better recognize and avoid this occurrence – unless we are trying to set it up to salvage a draw! In the diagram to the left, White has been restricting Black's moves, trying to fence him as in Diag. 3.1 of the preceding section. However, he has carelessly taken away all of Black's legal

47

moves. Remember Guideline 4 of the preceding section: *restrict the king to a box of only two possible squares and look for a mate*. Well, White has limited Black too much! Now it is Black to move but he has no where to move. Yet he is not in check. Therefore – because one cannot legally move *into* check – and he is not *in* check, the game is a draw by stalemate.

Stalemate does not have to be a result of a mistake, though. It is an honorable way to salvage a half point from a losing position. In the next diagram, Black's hopes of queening look dim and he is far behind in material. If things proceed normally, he will surely lose. Noticing how few moves he has, he spots a saving move: **1... Qf2+!** If White does not capture the queen, then White becomes the loser. So after the forced **2. Qxf**, we have the resulting stalemate in the diagram below.

#3.25 Black to move and try to draw by stalemate.

#3.26 After 1... Qf2+; 2. Qxf, Black escapes with a draw!

When the king is confined and you are running short on moves, look for possibilities of this type.

Remember: if you **keep your opponent in check**, then you don't have to worry about stalemating him!

Illustration of Other Draws

Insufficient winning material

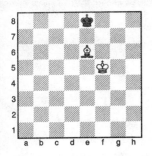

#3.27 Insufficient mating material.

#3.28 A mate cannot be *forced*.

#3.29 More than sufficient material!

Take special note of Diag. 3.29, insufficient mating material. Remember, the pawn is considered mating material because it has the possibility of transforming itself into mating force, such as a rook. This position should also serve as a reminder that if you are about to lose a game on time in which you are materially winning, then seek to destroy your opponent's last pawn to assure that you will at least draw the game even if your time does expire.

Draw by repetition of position

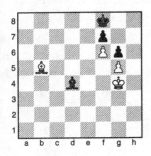

#3.30 Because White can't make any progress, he may as well continuously shift his bishop from b5 to a5.

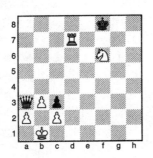

#3.31 Perpetual check is a form of repetition of position. White draws by checking from h7 or f6 (and even mates if Black goes to h8).

#3.32 Perpetual attacks on the White queen is being claimed as the repeated position. (It may be important whether White still has the castling option.)

50-move draw

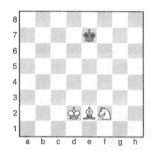

#3.33 Black can move aimlessly about for 50 moves, declare a draw, or move his pawn and stalemate White.

#3.34 A sure candidate for the 50-move rule at the scholastic level – but the mate can be accomplished in 35 moves. (Avoid White corners!)

#3.35 If Black is a weak computer, it may not concede a draw here. On the 49th move it may push the pawn so as to get another 50 moves in!

Note: The 175-move limit for a game was removed by the United States Chess Federation in 2003 when they released their 5th edition of the USCF's Official Rules of Chess.

Advancing in Chess: Unique and Characteristic Checkmates

Generally every mate will end in one of the mating patterns included here. Most of the patterns are distinct, but some are redundant and have been included simply because they are so common and need to be recognized instantly. You should learn the type of setups that spawn these mates and the conditions that make them possible. Three good books for this purpose are *Tal's Winning Chess Combinations* by Mikhail Tal and Victor Khenkin, *Power Mates* by Bruce Pandolfini, and *The Art of Attack in Chess* by Vukovic.

To demonstrate how multiplicative these patterns are, simply shift the positions to the queenside and you have "another" 25 positions. Too, you can make a switch of colors and set up a corresponding position from the other side, producing another 25 to 50. Not convinced? Well, switch the queen with the rook in the rook mates and you have several more; or swap the queen for the bishop and another series of related mates appear. To construct "new" back-rank mates, simply move the king up the board and prevent his backward movement either by restricting him with his own pieces or placing an enemy

50

rook one rank below the one occupied by the king. This creates a virtual back rank and allows you to then apply a characteristic mate. Use your imagination to duplicate these positions and see similarities. For instance, the "friendly" pawns in Diag. 3.37 serve the same function as the enemy king in Diag. 3.36 or the enemy rook on d7 of Diag. 3.38.

Major Piece Mates

#3.36 The common king-rook mate.

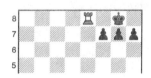

#3.37 Typical back-rank mate.

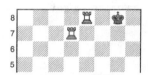

#3.38 The double-rook mate (two hogs feeding).

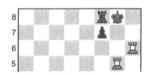

#3.39 A queen can replace one of the rooks.

#3.40 A queen could replace the rook.

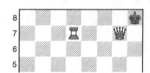

#3.41 The often seen queen-rook mate.

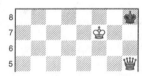

#3.42 Similar to a rook mate.

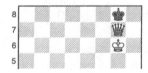

#3.43 The common king-queen mate.

#3.44 A regular mate.

#3.45 The common king-rook mate.

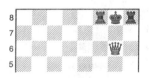

#3.46 The epaulette mate.

#3.47 A frequent guest at tournaments.

Minor-Piece Assisted Mates

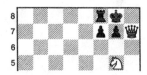

#3.48 The most common of the queen-knight mates.

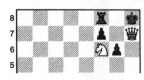

#3.49 A common queen-knight mate.

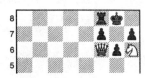

#3.50 Similar to a bishop-knight mate.

#3.51 The most frequent of the queen-bishop mates.

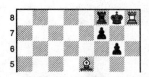

#3.52 A queen can replace the rook or bishop.

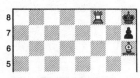

#3.53 A White pawn placed on h6 works, also.

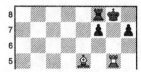

#3.54 A celebrated finale.

#3.55 A queen can replace the rook or pawn.

#3.56 One of the many knight-rook mates.

#3.57 The Arabian (rook-knight) mate.

#3.58 A common mate usually reached by sacrifices.

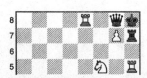

#3.59 Pinned pieces allow a spectrum of mates.

Minor-Piece Mates

#3.60 The most common of the smothered mates.

#3.61 A queen can replace the bishop.

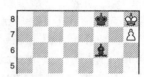

#3.62 A Black queen at f6 works, also.

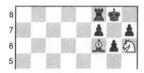

#3.63 The bishop-knight mate.

#3.64 A queen could replace the bishop.

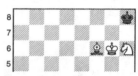

#3.65 A mate that may require 35 moves to set.

#3.66 A companion bishop-knight mate. This mate can occur on any square of the last rank.

#3.67 This opening may occur during the opening phase.

#3.68 The bishops sweep the diagonals.

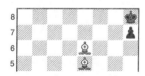

#3.69 A White pawn on f7 works, also.

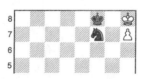

#3.70 An essential mate to know when reduced to only a knight.

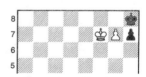

#3.71 A White bishop works similarly.

The set of mates cover practically every mating situation, with most other mating positions being simply a subset of these. In fact, even the "named" mates are just subsets of those that we have already characterized. For example, *Boden's Mate* (Diag. 3.72, below) is simply a version of the two-bishop mate illustrated in Diag. 3.68 and Diag. 3.69 of the previous page. (Rubinstein's Mate is also simply a two-bishop mate.) And *Anastasia's Mate* (Diag. 3.73), which comes from W. Heinse's novel *Anastasia and chess* (1803), represents the pattern of our given Diag. 3.58 of page 50.

It does not matter if you don't know the difference between the mating pattern of Morphy (Diag. 3.74) and Pillsbury (Diag. 3.75). Forget the tags. Just familiarize yourself with the illustrated mates of this section and try to reproduce them in your own games.

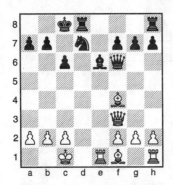

#3.72 Boden's Mate (White to Mate in 2)

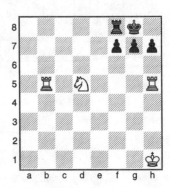

#3.73 Anastasia's Mate (White to Mate in 3)

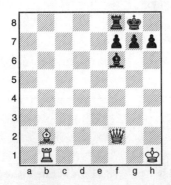

#3.74 Morphy's Mate (White to Mate in 3)

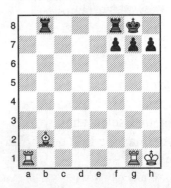

#3.75 Pillsbury's Mate (White to Mate in 3)

IV. Move Selection

Selecting Candidate Moves

If you are searching for a move and have no obvious attack points, then try to improve the position of your pieces. Please don't make pawn moves because you can't think of anything else to do. Identify what your worst-placed piece is and try to improve its position. In the meanwhile, perhaps your opponent will help you direct your focus by his subsequent moves. In evaluating to determine focus, look at (1) **material**, (2) **king safety**, and (3) who has the **initiative** (controls the play).

On the other hand, if you do have a target or are responding to a threat, select candidate moves to consider before you make a move on the board. You should select three likely moves to deal with a goal, analyze them one-at-a-time in your head, and then choose the best of the three moves as the most likely candidate move to actually make on the board. If none of the moves seem sufficient to answer the threat, then choose two more moves and analyze them. Because of time constraints you will probably not be able to conveniently analyze more than six or seven candidate moves per turn. (Computers analyze *all* possible moves before they select a move to play!) Once you have settled on a move, don't agonize over it. You may not have made the best move, but you will have chosen the best move of the moves you considered (based on your analytical ability).

Only after have chosen three good, likely moves do you begin to analyze whether they are strong, sound choices. Analyze them briefly, using no more than 30 seconds a move. If none are immediately eliminated, then analyze them more intensively, starting with the most promising move of the choices. Unless the analysis reveals a clearly decisive move, go to the next candidate. Do not try to force a move to work. If you have analyzed it twice, then it is generally not worth spending any more time on it. If none of the moves are sufficient, then select another candidate for evaluating. By selecting candidates before you play the first good looking move that you see, you'll arrive at the best move.

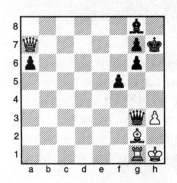

#4.1 Black to move – after choosing three candidates!

Let us see how we should apply this analytical method to form a decision based upon the diagram to the left. A **material valuation** shows that White has a rook to balance our three pawn advantage. Hmmm ... if I allow White to consolidate and perhaps get a little more active, I will be playing a whole rook down! Looking at **king safety** reveals that White is awfully close to being mated since his king is confined. And since it is Black's move, Black must have some sort of **initiative**. So the question is how to make the most of Black's position before White consolidates and starts attacking himself.

First of all, let's look at obvious threats. Black's a-pawn is under attack. White moving his bishop is no great threat because he can only safely move it to f1 as his weak pawn on h3 needs protecting. So our problem as Black is to keep White on the defensive.

Well, let's choose some candidate moves. My a-pawn might need some help, so: **(a) – Bc4**. I may be able to queen a pawn, so **(b) – f4**. I might want to queen the a-pawn, so **(c) – Qa3** is a likely candidate. Now let us analyze. **1... Bc4** looks okay. It protects the pawn and ensures that White can only draw if he plays Bf1. But what if he plays Qb6, threatening to pile up on g6 in the future? What if he simply moves Rc1 activating his rook with tempo or opening g1 to the queen for better defense of his king ? Well, I can't push my a-pawn but at least I might still be surviving. With nothing else more promising, this move may have to do.

What if I play **f4**? Then how will I counter Qxa or Qc7 with the threat of Rf1? Actually, I had thought this move might be good because I was threatening to hit the White Bishop with f4-f3, but simply Bf1 would be good because I can't even get a check in on f3 because of my own pawn! Worst still, if after 1... f4, 2. Qxa f3??; 3. Bf1 allows the rook to counter attack g6, causing immediate loss for Black! This variation certainly won't do!

What of **Qa3**? Well, Qf2 or Kh2 seem sufficient to free White up to attack. I think my queen is already in its best position. Not only that, before I got a chance to queen, I'd probably be mated!

So of my candidate moves looked at, Bc4 might have to do. However, since it is only the better of some poor alternatives, I'll look for something better. Whatever it is must be decisive and forcing, not allowing White time to consolidate. Only **g5**, **Qxh** and **Bd5** seem directly threatening. Okay, let's consider these alternatives.

Well, I can immediately dismiss **Qxh**? because of Bxh. No need hoping White will miss this forced and obvious reply. What of **g5**? Not bad. If after 1... g5 2. Qxa g4 3. hxg? Qh4! mates White! This might be the way! But what if he plays 3. Qe2! Then 3... gxh allows 4. Qh5 mate. Ugh. Well, suppose I play 3... Bf7, covering h5? Then 4. Qe1 covers all threats. Wow! That was close. I'll definitely play this if I can't find something better (since I am desperate) – just in case he does not see the forcing lines!

Okay, what of this **Bd5**? Well, suppose he just takes it: 2. Bxd? Whoa!! He can't just take it because the White bishop is needed to defend h3. Hold on, here! This is the move. If he captures my bishop, I mate him by taking on h3. If he moves his rook, then Qxg2 mates. And on most other moves by White Qxh3 delivers mate because the White bishop is *pinned* along the diagonal to the king!

So by using candidate moves, we have selected the best move to be played on the board. This time we found a strong, winning move. Had we made a so-so move, we may have been left praying for a draw. So, select candidate moves, evaluate the candidates, then choose the best one of the candidates to make on the board. Note that had we been short of time we may have settled for 1... Bc4 as the best of some bad choices and entirely missed the winning 1... Bd5.

Because the technique of choosing candidate moves will be useful throughout your entire chess career and is crucial to learning how to evaluate a position, let us work another example using this methodology. (Another example of candidate move application can be found in Section 5 – combinations – on page 70.)

The following successive positions resulted from a game that I played with Black against an expert in a club game.

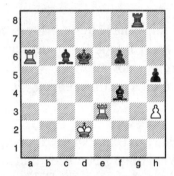

#4.2 Selecting candidate moves for Black.

#4.3 Of many winning variations, Black seeks to find the best move.

A quick evaluation of Diag. 4.2 shows that Black has an attack (the initiative) as well as a material advantage. Because Black's king is safe and it is his move, it is obvious that Black should win. It is now just a matter of finding the best winning method. Let us choose some candidate moves. Since the rook on e3 is pinned in Diag. 4.2, let's use it for a focus because it is good to pile pressure on pinned pieces. **Re8** and **Rg3** immediately suggest themselves. Too, the simple **Bxe3** is certainly a viable candidate move.

Now let us analyze. **1... Re8**; 2. Ra3 and now rook or bishop takes. Well, what of **1... Rg3**? This is actually better than the previous variation. For after the forced 2. Ra3 we have Rxh3 with the same choices but we are up a pawn. So forget variation one – this latter variation is for choice. Now what of **Bxe3**? Not bad. After 2. Kxe Rg3+ ; 3. K any Rxh. This is almost as good as the last variation. What I don't particularly like about it is that White still has a rook on that could complicate things. Black should certainly win but it could be a tough win. Well, I think that Rg3 should be my selected move. In this case it is no need to look for other moves because this move is so strong.

After **1... Rg3; 2. Ra3 Rxe!; 3. Rxe** we get Diag. 4.3 above. I played 2... Rxe because I wanted to maintain the pin on the rook. So I actually choose this move from two other candidate moves: 1. Rxh and Bxe. Now let us consider the options from Diag. 4.3. I can try to bring my king up to increase pressure on the pin with **Kd5**. I can fix the h-pawn on white by playing **h4**. I can kill his rook with **Bxe+**.

Actually nothing is wrong with this immediate move, for sure. **1... Bxe**; 2. Kxe Ke5 with a slow but sure win in sight. Better than this, though, would be to save a tempo and immediately begin setting up the attack on the a-pawn with **1... h4**. Now if 2. Ke2 Bxe; 3. Kxe Bg2. Nice enough and leads to a much quicker win than variation one. And **1... Kd5**? Well, it simply seems to waste a move, for if he moves his king I must take his rook anyway. **1... Kd5**; 2. Ke2 Bxe; 3. Kxe Ke5.

But wait, suppose in this last line he plays 2. Kd3 instead of 2. Ke2? Then 2... Bb5+ would allow me to win the whole rook because I can get my king to Kd4 and double attack it. Based on this assessment, it occurred to me that 1... **Bb5** may, itself, be a decent candidate move!

So let us look at 1... Bb5. Hey! White has only one move to keep from losing his rook! After **1... Bb5**; 2. h4 Kd5 White must simply abandon his rook to my bishop. So instead of simply winning the h-pawn, the use of candidate moves has resulted in me winning a whole rook! This is the beauty of candidate moves: they allow you to consider moves that you might not play because of other plausible options.

Before you move, ask: "WHY?"

The use of candidate moves will help you choose the best move. However, in scholastic chess the players seem to be in a hurry to make any move that is at all plausible. They simply miss the attacks of their opponents. In scholastic chess, one-move blunders are pervasive. For the first five or six years that I started teaching chess, I concentrated on trying to show players how to recognize and construct combinations. It soon became apparent to me that this strategy was only useful for more advanced students. Hence it behooves you as a student or coach to try to reduce one-move blunders before moving to combinations. It does not matter that Johnny can solve 5-move mates when he is constantly overlooking one-move attacks on his queen.

Therefore, I devised a stratagem to deal with this problem. I originally used a mnemonic called **TOP COP** Stops Flops (see the Appendix for a handout).

The "T" stood for **Threats**, the first "O" stood for the **Opponent's** doings, and the first "P" for **Plans**. You first look for direct threats and then plans of your opponent. The "C" stands for **Checks** and **Captures**, the last "O" for **Our** doings – emphasizing things that we should try to do, and the last "P" for **Patterns**. You first look for direct attacks that you might have and then see if any themes are emerging, such as smothered mate. After teaching *Top Cop* for years, the methodology simplified and evolved into *WHY?*, which concentrates upon the opponent's threats. Thus the following stratagem is useful for getting players to look at immediate problems and opportunities, focusing on the move.

Before you move, ask: "WHY?"

Why did he choose that move?
> What pieces are now attacked?
> Is his move part of a plan?

Does the move help me?
> Did he give me some threats?
> Did his move create weaknesses?

Now let us see how this stratagem can be used to reduce blunders and direct your play. We will follow Black's thinking in the following situation. White has a choice of captures in Diag. 4.4, below. What White would prefer to do is capture on d4 with his queen and set up a position as in Diag. 4.5. But White recaptured on d4 with a pawn (Diag. 4.6). Why did he choose that particular move over 1. Qxd4 which would have brought his Queen to an aggressive post with attack on Black's center as well as kingside pressure?

#4.4 How should White recapture?

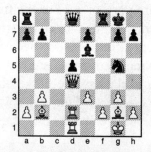

#4.5 White's dream.

#4.6 White's choice. Why?

Let us first deal with Diag. 4.6. Asking the first question *What pieces are now attacked?* shows that *our* knight is under attack. We'll have to deal with that direct threat before considering any other moves. Before we move, though, let us ask *Is his move part of a plan?* Well, maybe he is just quickly liberating his black-square bishop. Or maybe he is planning on piling up pressure on the e-pawn which is now backward on an open file. His plan may not be obvious, but his attack on the knight is real. So after first checking to make sure *that he did not give me any stronger threats than his threat* to capture my knight, I move my knight out of harm's way (most strongly to h3). As far as weaknesses, he actually did create one with his move: the isolated d-pawn. But I'll have to deal with that later!

Now suppose he had instead captured with his queen (Diag. 4.7). *What pieces are now attacked?* Well, our d-pawn is now double-attacked. As far as *Is his move part of a plan?*, we already showed his hope in Diag. 4.5. Before we rush to defend, let us now ask *Did he give me some threats?* and *Did his move create weaknesses?* In fact, White did give us a threat by removing protection from the f3 square. An alert Black would see that 1... Nf6+ attacks the king and queen, forcing the White bishop to give itself up *and* simultaneously giving defense to the Black queen pawn. Now after 2. BxN RxB, Black has obtained White's strong Bishop.

#4.7 What threats could Qxd have given Black?

Before you gloat though, your forced moves now gives White an attack on *your* d-pawn with 3. Rd1. But this gives Black, in turn, an attack on *White's* f-pawn with 3... Qf8! The moves are there – and you can find them if you but ask **WHY?**

Only after the "WHY?" assessment should one scan the board for targets to attack, looking first at all checks, immediate attacks, and unprotected pieces. **COACHES** (and students): A fuller exposition of this method of questioning and move evaluation is presented in the Appendix. There a comprehensive methodology is given that will help chess players select moves and virtually eliminate one-move errors – if followed. It evolved from the "WHY?" stratagem and should be the basis that maturing players routinely use to guide their play. The methodology is based upon: (1) responding to threats, (2) seeking one's own threats, (3) simply improving one's position if no immediate threats are available, and (4) using candidate moves to determine the better choices. Days can be spent drilling with this method.

Advancing in Chess: Tactical Development

Books for Tactical Development

There are many books that have been written on how to construct chess combinations and increase one's analytical ability. Learning to analyze deeply (3 or more moves) is essential for advancement in chess. In fact, it is in the area of tactical prowess that experts most distinguish themselves from average players. The good news is that study of tactical positions will increase our tactical awareness and ability. Again, these books have been arranged in order of their user-friendliness or usefulness for establishing a basis for more advanced treatments. Try to get the more recent publications – if any!

1001 Brilliant Chess Sacrifices and Combinations, Fred Reinfeld, Bell Publishing Co., New York, 1969. A compilation of chess combinations, mates, and surprising moves. The diagrams are presented without comments but grouped by theme. This is a very useful and inexpensive book for self-study which encourages solving the positions directly from the diagrams. Even 800-level players will find material here to train their solving ability. This book is now available free online in pdf-format or as an e-book. (Try chessville.com.)

Bobby Fischer's Outrageous Chess Moves, Bruce Pandolfini, Simon & Schuster, Inc., New York, 1985. This is a study of 101 chess combinations by the past World Chess Champion. The clues to the positions and solutions are presented on the same page with the diagram. A nice touch is the inclusion of the actual games in an appendix. If one solves the position by transferring them to a chess board for study, players at any level up to expert level can use this book for advancement.

Tal's Winning Chess Combinations, Mikhail Tal and Victor Khenkin, Scripta Publishing Co., New York, 1979. An excellent book for training one's tactical ability and pattern recognition. Most classic mating patterns and combinations are first presented and then treated with examples of increasing difficulty. It is probably the best book available for leading one from the simple to the complex and developing tactical skills. It is most appropriate for USCF ratings of 1200 – 1900.

Art of Attack in Chess, Vladimir Vukovic, Cadogan Books, London, 1998. This highly-touted books is worthy of its reputation. It abounds with attacks on the king, illustrating: (1) the pattern that you should visualize and focus your moves on, (2) the prerequisites for a successful attack based on the pattern, and (3) many classic examples of realizing the pattern or variants. It is an excellent presentation that even 1300-level players can appreciate.

Think Like a Grandmaster, Alexander Kotov, Batsford, London, 1978. This book trains you to consider pertinent choices before you make your move on the board. It is the how-to book of candidate moves, and introduces the analysis tree to promote its message. It is designed to train anyone to improve at move selection. However, you will probably have to be 1500 strength or stronger to really grasp the material.

Online Resources for Tactical Development

The Internet has revolutionized the study of tactics. A multitude of free sites presents tens of thousands of puzzles for your daily consumption. And some of these sites present these tactical problems in an interactive format: you make a move and the computer supplies a response. Too, many of these sites assess your tactical ability and grade you based on the puzzles' difficulty or other user's responses based on average time-to-solution and chess rating. Providing a personal rating and charting your growth in tactical strength is a powerful method of encouraging one to continue to apply themselves to tactics daily. Another selling point of these free resources is that you can request a particular theme (such as discovered check, smothered mate, etc.) and thus quicken your mastery of a particular tactic.

Practically every one of the hundreds of chess sites provides a free daily tactical puzzle. One of the best free sites for tactical growth is the **Chess Tactics Server** (chess.emrald.net). Its interactivity almost places it in the realm of a video game. And its extremely fast server allows you to solve a puzzle per minute–or more, depending upon your ability. It gives you instant feedback on how you compare with others who have attempted the puzzle and maintains your rating onsite to chart your progress.

Another very popular free site is **Chess Tempo** (chess.tempo.com). It is similar to the Chess Tactics Server but is geared more toward personal progress, presenting graphs of your successes and weaknesses as well as allowing you to target tactics by theme or need. The problems presented on Chess tempo are mostly of the move-to-win variety with fewer actual mates been presented. Too, there is less concentration on speedy calculation, so the problems can be solved like an over-the-board challenge in a tournament game with a slow time rate. Chess Tempo is more a full-suite site since it also has a chess computer that you can challenge as well a database of over 2 million games.

Ideachess (www.ideachess.com) is a free chess tactics training site that aims to help chess-lovers improve their game by solving online interactive checkmate and chess tactics puzzles. The main distinguishing features of Ideachess is a real-time tactical chess engine that immediately refutes wrong solutions. The site has over 40,000 tactical problems arranged by theme and checkmate. You are allowed to track your tactical progress with graphs and charts. Another distinguishing feature is that the site can assign tactical problems to you based on your rating, thus challenge you on your level of expertise. Ideachess also lets you challenge its computer on different levels.

And here we switch into the paid sites. The Tactics Trainer at chess.com is very useful for tactical development but does charge a nominal free for its usage if you want to solve more than ten problems a day. On a whole, the problems are a little more difficult than those served up on Chess Tempo or the Chess Tactics Server. Further, there are the multitudes of pay-for-use sites such as the Internet Chess Club (chessclub.com). It has everything for your daily chess growth but is certainly more costly. However, if you are an aspiring chess player who wants to be competitive, you will find that it is worth the cost.

Whatever your choice, don't neglect the internet chess sites as a tool for your tactical growth. Too, don't be concerned that the above-mentioned free sites may phase out or become pay-to-play sites in the future because there will certainly be many similar free sites being developed to attract chess players. Search out the sites and register at multiple sites to take advantage of the differing tools that they offer.

V. Middlegame: Combinations

Defining a combination

A definition proposed by several modern grandmasters for a combination is: "... *a sacrifice combined with a forced sequence of moves, which exploits specific peculiarities of the position in the hope of attaining a certain goal.*" Here *peculiarities* pertain to factors such as a vulnerable king, undefended pieces, or inadequately defended pieces. The goal of a combination could be to win material, mate the opponent, or simply ward off an attack. For our purposes, we should think of a combination in terms of Emanuel Lasker's (an early World Champion) definition: "*A variation or net of variations which leads to a desirable issue by force.*" So let us regard a combination as a sequence of two or more consecutive moves which enables us to forcefully achieve an aim.

Let us see how a combination comes about. Consider Diag. 5.1 below. From prior knowledge, White is acquainted with this mate (see page 41). In Diag. 5.2, White attacks d8 twice and Black defends the square once. Hence 1. Rxd+

#5.1 Our goal.   **#5.2 White wins with Rxd8+.**

Rxd; 2. Rxd++ leads to the mate of Diag. 5.1. Though White combined two moves to achieve his goal, most consider this an exchange rather than a combination. Yet by Lasker's definition it would be considered a combination.

In Diag. 5.3 (next page), White attacks d8 twice and it is defended twice. Hence if White captures the rook on d8, Black simply captures with his rook

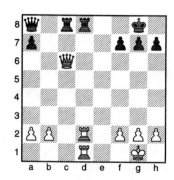

#5.3 White has a combination.

and survives. But White reasons that if he can reduce Black's defenders, then he can achieve the same mate as in Diag. 5.1. Hence he plays the "combination" of **1. Qxa Rxa** (now we have Diag. 5.2); **2. Rxd+ Rxd; 3. Rxd++**. We will regard the exchange in Diag. 5.3 as a combination (using a sequence of forced moves to achieve a goal). Strictly speaking, though, in higher-level chess this would not be touted as a combination unless we swap the position of the Black queen and rook in Diag. 5.3 and then begin the sequence with Qxa, sacrificing material (queen for rook) to achieve our goal.

At the scholastic chess level, we aim to be practical. We should have no concern for the semantics of a real combination. If we foresee the outcome of a forced series of exchanges, then I think we should proudly label it a combination! So let's demystify the jargon now and see combinations as something that any scholastic player should be able to play.

The Tactics of Combinations

In early 1900's, the chess master Teichmann stated that *chess is 99% tactics.* This assessment has not changed much today. The largest difference between masters and amateurs is their command of tactics. Thankfully, tactics can be learned. Indeed, tactical training is where most beginners can realize the greatest improvement in their game – and, consequently, this is where their emphasis should be! There are several methods which can be used to increase one's tactical competence: (1) playing against players who are higher-rated than yourself, (2) studying the games of great players, learning how they won and made their pieces cooperate, (3) playing computers set at a higher level than your present strength, (4) solving chess problems similar to the diagrams presented in this section, and (5) analyzing your own games with the help of a stronger player or a computer. This latter method will reveal the many routine tactical shots that occur in your own games and are overlooked! Now let us look at tactics in action: combinations.

Combinations are based upon weaknesses ("peculiarities of the position"). To identify the presence of a combination, first assess the strengths and weaknesses of the position. Are there loose pieces, weak squares, checks on the king, possible attacks on more valuable pieces by relatively less-valued pieces, or any trace of recognizable themes or patterns present (such as back-rank mate or smothered mate) in the position? If none of these elements are present, then perhaps they can be created. Seeing nothing concrete, you now enter the "what-if" or fantasy mode: "If my piece could get to this or that square, then it would threaten this; if his piece were not there, then this square would be weak and I could start an attack; if this pawn were out of the way, I could get in a devastating check; or if he did not defend that piece, then I could set up a double attack." Work from the obvious to the fantasy-based plan.

Just what are these signposts that should signal the presence of a combination? The following table of twelve signals should prompt you to look for a combination. If the list seems too much at first, then simply remember to look at – before you move – **all possible checks, undefended pieces, and attacks of lesser-valued pieces on higher-valued ones**. Such a quick look will alert you to the scent of perhaps 80% of possible combinations.

Indications of Combinations

Unsafe King	• presence of checks
	• uncastled king
	• cramped king position
	• weakened castled position (protectors absent or pawn structure weakened)
	• preponderance of pieces in a section
Vulnerable Pieces	• pinned pieces
	• unprotected pieces
	• double attacks and pieces that can be forked (knight fork, pawn fork, etc.)
	• pieces which are stalemated or can't readily retreat
	• overworked defenders (divert or deflect)
Known Methods	• pawns nearing promotion (6th or 7th rank)
	• traces of known themes

Looking at the list, note how attacks against the king and higher-valued pieces comprise most of the list. The first five items all pertain to the **king's safety**. Item 5 requires some explanation, though. If you have got a preponderance of pieces *aimed* (they don't have to actually be on the squares in the sector – just controlling them) at the side where the opponent is castled, then you can spare some of them to weakened his castled position by sacrificing them. Too, it doesn't matter that he has a knight and rook protecting the king when you have, say, two bishops, a knight, rook, and queen attacking – you might have two or more pieces which can be sacrificed!.

The next five items of the list deal with **direct threats and attack**. This is why you should always ask what is attacked – or can be attacked – before you move. Item 11, pawn promotion, is actually another type of direct attack. This time, though, it is a direct attack on a square rather than a piece. If you have more attackers on the promotion square than the defender has controllers, then you can successfully queen.

Item 12 is more a generalized attack or pattern-recognition attack. ("I saw Kasparov do something like this in one of his games.") The more themes you know (such as back-rank mate, triangulation, rooks on the 7th, double-bishop sacrifice, bishop sacrifices on h7 or h2, bishop-knight mate, etc.), then the more of these possibilities you will become aware of during a game. (Read books and review master-level games to learn more of these themes.)

The presence of checks (Item 1) and double attacks (Item 8) comprise the bulk of all combinations. (Note that pins are a form of double attack, attacking one piece through another.) Once you become more practiced, pattern recognition and traces of known themes will be the mainstay of your combinations against good opponents. The really nice thing about learning is that the more you play, the patterns that you recognize will be things that you, yourself, have played!

Now don't sit around waiting for these signposts to appear. If you don't detect a possible combination, then simply try to improve the placement of your pieces. In due time you will get a strong enough position that a combination will be possible. Too, there is always the possibility that your opponent will blunder and present you with an opportunity. So get your pieces in position to take advantage of appearing weaknesses. This means developing your rooks onto files which may later be opened and maximizing the range of your pieces.

Using the listing of signposts, try to solve the positions at the end of this section and describe which of the elements of the itemized list pertain to them. The "Mate in **x**" positions are derived from known chess games – again emphasizing the need for one to study the great games of the past. Moreover, because the "Mate in **x**" positions involve mates, don't bother to list the presence of checks as a signpost for those particular diagrams. All forced mates aren't labeled. **White moves first in all diagrams.** (The answers to the diagrams are included in the Appendix.)

Because one does "play as they practice," it is advisable to reproduce the diagrams on a chess board before you proceed to work them. Then ask yourself what advantages White has. Try to identify some of the signs or motifs of the combinations. Next, propose some candidate moves to achieve your objective. Then work out the combinations in your head as if you were playing over-the-board. The more you simulate real play, the more value you will derive from the positions.

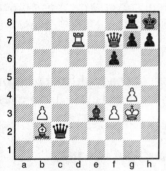

#5.4 In an Internet game, White searches for a kill.

Before you start solving the following diagrams, let's demonstrate how one should approach a problem position. Using the diagram to the left, we should first take a **material balance**. Material is equal. Next we would consider **king and piece safety** (*always look for checks and loose pieces!*). White's king is more exposed than Black's. In fact, White appears to be in serious trouble. Not only that, the bishop at b2 can prove difficult to defend. But wait! Let us not forget **who has the initiative**: it is White to move so he controls the subsequent play. This changes everything. With the move White may be able to set up a defense.

Still, it will be tough defending f3 and the bishop at b2!

Well, let us see if any combinational motifs are present. Yes there are: Black's position presents a check on the move (Item 1), has a cramped king position (Item 3), a relative scarcity of pieces at the king's house (Item 5), and there are some traces of tactical weaknesses in his position (Item 12) – specifically, ideas of pins radiating from f6 and back rank mates.

69

Now let us propose some moves that will deal with the problem of defending our weak kingside and unprotected piece as well as forcefully attacking Black before he can take advantage of our weaknesses. Moving the bishop out of harm's way seems plausible. And since we want to do something forcing, I will consider **1. Bxf**. For that matter, why not 1. **Qxf**, since it defends the Bishop and my weakened kingside? Well, because I must do something forcing and there are elements of known tactical themes present, let me also consider **1. Qxg+** while I am looking at candidate moves! Enough candidates. Now to some concrete analysis.

I'd like to play **1. Bxf!?** gxf?; 2. Qxf+ Rg7; 3. Qxg++ or Rd8++. However, if I slowly proceed Black can himself win with 1... Qf2+; 2. Kh3 Qxf+. It is obvious that White must do something very forcing or else he will lose. Well, **1. Qxf!?** sets up the same sort of mate while defending the bishop and f3! But, alas, Black can sneak in a perpetual check with 1. Qxf Qf2+; 2. Kh3 Qf1+; 3. Kh2 Qg1+, etc. Maybe he can even get his own mate in! No matter: giving up the draw is undesirable enough to prompt me to analyze my other candidate move. Wow! There is great potential here if we simply reverse the move order of our first planned assault: **1. Qxg+** Rxg; 2. Rd8+ Rg8; 3. Bxf++. Now we boldly plop this combination down on the board!

Note that I had to know the back rank mating pattern of Diag.5.1 (first page of this section) and about pins. And more importantly – before I evaluated moves or made a move, I selected candidate moves.

Candidate move evaluation and combinations go hand in hand.

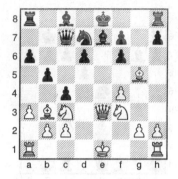

#5.5   Layers of combinations.

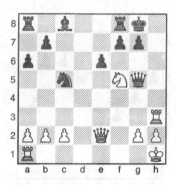

#5.6   Mate in three.

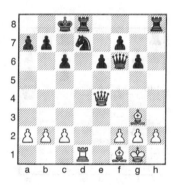

#5.7   Bishop sweep.

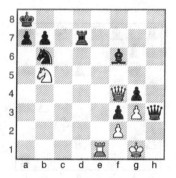

#5.8   Thematic mate.

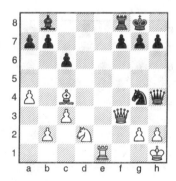

#5.9   Weakened back rank.

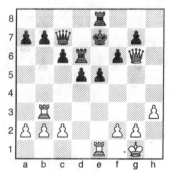

#5.10   A skewer beats a pin.

#5.11   Win by diversion.

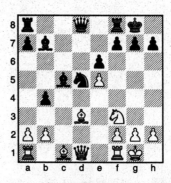

**#5.12   Standard Bh7 sac.
Analyze it to learn it.**

#5.13   Mate in four.

#5.14   Mate in three.

#5.15   Family problems.

#5.16   Mate in three.

#5.17 Mate in four.

#5.18 Mate in three.

#5.19 Mate in six.

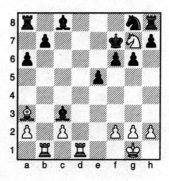

#5.20 Mate in five.

#5.21 Fork it over!

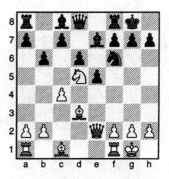

#5.22 Doubling up.

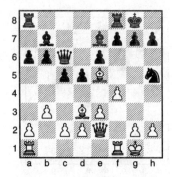

#5.23 Lasker's classic game.

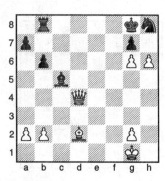

#5.24 Devastating pins.

#5.25 The power of the king.

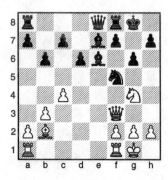

#5.26 Knowing themes helps.

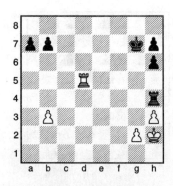

#5.27 Mouse trap!

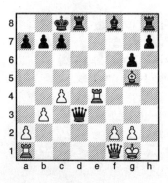

#5.28 Unprotected piece.

Advancing in Chess: Middlegame Considerations

Books Explaining Strategy

The following books have proved themselves invaluable for the advancement of all chess players and are especially useful for self-study and improvement. Don't worry that some of them seem ancient – just hope that there is a current publication of it. The books are listed in what I perceive to be either their order of usefulness or simpleness, with either the easiest to comprehend or the ones most needed to establish a foundation being listed first.

Pawn Structure Chess, Andrew Soltis, David McKay Co., NY, 1995. You need to understand the chess position before you can stage your pieces to attack your opponent. *"Much of the strategic potential in a chess game hinges on the distinct pawn formations reached after the first ten or so moves."* This book profiles each of these formations and shows you how to play them.. Many pertinent games are chosen to illustrate how to treat specific pawn and piece placements. This excellent development is good for 1200+ players, laying a foundation for positional understanding.

Test Your Positional Play, Robert Bellin and Pietro Ponzetto, Macmillan Publishing Co., New York, 1985. This book tackles the problem of how to improve middlegame success by showing players how to analyze a position, form objectives, and establish a plan.   Thirty graded tests of increasing complexity are presented to enable the student to progress. Candidate moves are proposed, and the preferred moves are reinforced with actual play from the game. You can also get an estimate of your rating by comparing your score with that of other USCF-rated players.

Best Lessons of a Chess Coach, Sunil Weeramantry and Ed Eusebi, McKay Chess Library, NY, 1993. Ten games are presented as lessons and throughly analyzed with focus on perhaps the 1500-level. However, the themes presented and excellent coverage of the book can be useful to anyone from the 1200 – 1900 level because of the supportive text and excellent explanation. Challenging questions and answers add much instructive value. Outpost squares, weak-color complexes, sacrifices for the initiative, and material imbalances are some of the material covered.

The Middlegame, Book One: Static Features, M. Euwe and H. Kramer, Hayes Publishing, Dallas, TX, 1994. A compilation of decades of instructive games (about 500 in total with Book Two) which illustrate middlegame features that are static, such as the value of the pieces, open and closed formations, file control, and plans based upon pawn structure. Because the elements considered are static, the material of the book is forever relevant and valuable.

The Middlegame, Book Two: Dynamic and Subjective Features, M. Euwe and H. Kramer, Hayes Publishing, Dallas, TX, 1994. A complement to the afore-mentioned Book One, this game collection treats dynamic features of chess such as time considerations, the initiative, maneuvering, psychological factors, and personal style in conducting attacks. This is the book that you need to study if you are more a tactician than positional player.

Modern Chess Strategy, Ludek Pachman, Dover, New York, 1979. Minority attack, minor piece valuation and placement, heavy piece activity, equilibrium – explanation and illustration of these aspects of general chess strategy make this book a must. This book shows how one should use strategic principles to promote combinational opportunities.

Resources Illustrating Good Play with Instructional Value

Complete games are the best source of middlegame training because they demonstrate how all the aspects of the game must be coordinated to help you realize your objectives and produce a win. Many good books on specific players have been published, and I advise you to read those of the players whose style appeal to you. Too, don't neglect the valuable annotated games that appear in *Chess Life & Review*, the USCF's magazine. The game collections recommended here have instructional value based upon their historical value and clear presentation.

Most Instructive Games of Chess Ever Played: 62 Masterpieces of Chess Strategy, Irving Chernev, Simon & Shuster, New York, 1965. This book presents some of the most important games ever played with excellent notation. The clear and instructive notation emphasizes unchanging opening tips, middlegame considerations, and endgame principles. The book demonstrates how masters coordinate their pieces to realize the theory of chess in actual combat.

Zurich International Chess Tournament, 1953, David Bronstein, General Publishing Co., Canada, 1979. The games of one of the most important tournaments ever played – where essentially all of the leading masters of the chess era played – are presented with excellent notation. Bronstein coaches you through many of the games and provides explanation that even 1200-level players can appreciate as well as concepts that masters should try to emulate. I add my voice to those who proclaim this as the best tournament book ever written. The intrinsic quality of the games are heighten through the quality of the annotations and passion of the interpreter.

Today, computer programs and the Internet provide a valuable tool for developing your middlegame. You can pull multiple games from a database that illustrate a theme (such as the minority attack) and quickly play these games out using a computer that is assisted by a chess engine to give you instant feedback on the evaluation of a variation. Free online databases also can be used to supplement your development in the middlegame. With sites like *Ideachess*, *Chess Tempo*, and *Chessbase* providing huge databases of games, you can play through current games and rapidly explore strategical ideas being implemented over-the-board by top grandmasters.

VI. Endgame

Endgame Principles

The paramount principle of the endgame is: **try to identify your advantage and form a plan on how to realize it – try to visualize the end position that you feel will yield the strongest position.** Some general guidelines applicable to endgames are given below and will be expanded upon to give you practical examples of how to proceed in the endgame.

1. The king is a fighting piece (worth ~3 points) and should be centralized and actively used.
2. Try to gain tempi whenever possible.
3. Push passed pawns as soon as feasible and as far as practical.
4. Place rooks behind passed pawns.
5. The fewer the pieces, the more important the pawns.
6. Steer for flexible, sound pawn formations.
7. The outside passed pawn is an advantage.
8. Hold on to your material advantage. Sacrifice pawns for development only to activate a passive Rook.
9. In open or semi-open positions, Bishop are superior to Knights.
10. Knights are superior to Bishops in blocked positions.

Good technique wins endgame. Five of the main guidelines are: (1) establish a clear plan and follow it, (2) avoid complications, (3) don't allow counter play, (4) hold on to material, and (5) be both careful and patient. (An advanced concept which you should validate yourself as your skill grows is: To win an "even" endgame, you must give your opponent two weaknesses.)

Countless games are lost by beginners simply because they do not use their king as a piece. In minor piece endgames, use of the king is equivalent to use of a bishop or knight. If you have your king safely tucked away in a corner, then you are playing a piece down!

In Diag. 6.1, next page, White has emerged from a stormy middlegame two pawns up. But because his king is badly placed (and Black has the move), he will lose the endgame. Black simply gobbles the White queenside pawns and queens his own. Similarly, the Black king wins from Diag. 6.2 easily with 1... Kc3, winning the knight and either using his b-pawn as a decoy to get to the White pawns on the kingside or simply queening the b-pawn (best).

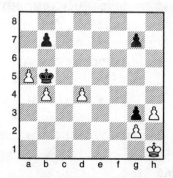

#6.1 The king is a fighting piece.

#6.2 The king overpowers a knight.

In Diag. 6.3 below, White demonstrates good technique by using the pin on the knight to gain tempi. After **1. Be4 g6; 2. Bd5 f6; 3. Kc2 Kb8** (See Diag. 6.4 where White realizes that he has weakened Black enough to win without need of the bishop. So he swaps pieces to limit Black's potential counter play with the knight.); **4. Bxb Kxb; 5. Kd3 Kc7; 6. Kc4 Kc6; 7. h4 f5 8. g3 h6; 9. f3 g5; 10. h5 g4 11. f4** and Black is in zugswang and so loses his a-pawn.

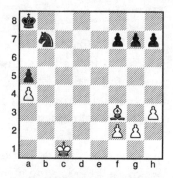

#6.3 Principles 1, 2, and 9 in play. White to move.

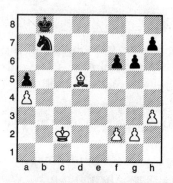

#6.4 After Kb8, the bishop has served its purpose.

In Diag. 6.5 (next page), White demonstrates how to prevent counter play and use the king as a fighting piece. **1. Rd3** Playing the rook back so that the pawn

#6.5 In Najdorf vs Kottnauer, White prevents counter play.

can give it support to oppose penetration by the Black rook. **1... Ke6 2. Kf3 Rc8** (g6 better) **3. Rc3 Rd8** (Black can't afford to swap rooks while a pawn down.); **4. Re3+ Kf6; 5. Rd3 Rc8; 6. Rc3 Rd8; 7. Rc6+** and wins. (However, 7. Rc7 allows 7... Rd2, which will exchange queenside pawns.)

Principle 8, *sacrificing pawns to activate a rook*, is so important that it deserves a much larger discussion. However, this may be an advanced topic for beginning scholastic players so it has been included in the Appendix (*Sacrificing for Active Rook Play*).

Pawn Promotion

Now we get to the topic that dominates most endgames: pawn promotion. Pawns are the lowest valued of all pieces – until they reach the last rank. If a pawn reaches the eight rank (the last one of your opponent), it can promote to any piece other than another pawn or a king. Hence you can possibly have nine queens on the board at the same time. (Watch out for stalemate!) Since one most often promotes such a proud pawn to a queen, the highest valued piece, this operation is often called *queening*. There are many ways that a pawn can thread himself through the maze of opponent's pieces and pawns but most of them are related to the themes of outrunning the pieces of the enemy or overwhelming the defense.

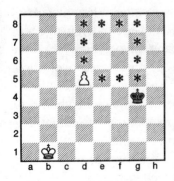

#6.6 Square of the pawn.

Two good rules to know when facing pawns trying to queen are: (1) keep your king inside the *"square of the pawn,"* and (2) place your rooks *behind* passed pawns (your own or your opponents). In Diag. 6.6 (to the left) if it is Black to move, he draws by playing his king inside the square of the pawn (any of the starred squares).

The square of the pawn is determined by counting the number of squares from the square – *and*

81

including the square – upon which the pawn sits to the last rank where it queens. And, next, counting an equal number of squares to the side of the pawn, forming a square. (Alternatively, you can determine the square of the pawn by mentally drawing a line diagonally from the square upon which the pawn sits to the last rank and then squaring this projection out. In the Diag. 6.6, the diagonal line runs from d5 to g8.) Be careful not to overlook that pawns can go two squares on their first move! For pawns starting on their respective second ranks, consider them as being on their third rank before you start mapping their square. Now, if the opposing king is inside the square, he can stop the pawn if it has more than one square to go before queening – regardless of whose move it is. In Diag. 6.6 (previous page), White wins if it is his move; Black draws on the move by moving to f5 or g5.

#6.7 The knight is safe.

In Diag. 6.7 Black is helpless. If he captures the knight, he leaves the square of the pawn; otherwise, the White king eats the h-pawn and then assists with the promotion of his b-pawn. Note that if the knight were on d6, Black could capture the knight and draw since he would remain within the square of the pawn.

Using the square-of-the-pawn methodology can aid you in determining whether an unassisted pawn can be overtaken by an enemy king. But though the application of the concept can help you quickly visually determine the outcome of a pawn race, the concept is not always useful to help you avoid counting errors. In some positions you simply must count to determine whether queening is feasible. For instance, in Diag. 6.8, the square-of-the-pawn usage won't help much in assessing the position. A count is necessary. And it will reveal that even though Black can capture the a-pawn and queen first, he still will lose the game. Hence he should play Kc4!, using the opposition to eventually win White's f-pawn and preventing the White king from charging up the board and counter-attacking his abandoned kingside.

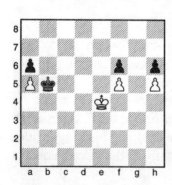

#6.8 Black to move and use counting.

82

Now let's investigate the second concept: rooks belong behind passed pawns. If your rook is behind your pawn, then it need not move again to support the advance of the pawn. Moreover, each advance of the pawn gives your rook an additional rank upon which to operate. So, each advance of your pawn strengthens your rook. On the other hand, if your rook is in front of your passer, each advance of the pawn restricts the available space of the rook. If your rook is behind your opponent's pawn, it becomes stronger with each advance of the pawn. If your rook is in front of the pawn, each advance of the pawn decreases your rook's maneuverability. Therefore – if you are forced to be in front of the enemy pawn – blockade the pawn as soon as possible, ideally on the 6th rank. In fact, note how a speedy blockade of the pawn with a rook at, say a6, renders a defender's rook at a8 inactive (Diag. 6.9).

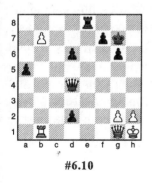

#6.9 White's rook is not ideally placed, but an early blockade grants it activity.

Now to the tactics of queening. Diag. 6.10 (below) illustrates the most common forms of queening: with Black to move, he first eliminates a defender (with Qxg1) and then queens; if White is to move, he can simply push his passer since the queening square is guarded by his rook. (If there was no pawn on h2, White couldn't win even though he queened first – *check* it out!) Diag. 6.11 (Black to move) shows a most common tactic, removing the guard. With Rxh, Black captures White's passer and ensures that only he will be queening. Diag. 6.12 shows the effectiveness of getting pawns abreast (White to move). White crashes through with Bxe, though Bh3-g2-c6 also wins. The endgame principal exemplified here is that two un-attacked pawns on the sixth rank are worth a rook.

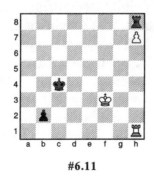

#6.10

#6.11

#6.12

Diag. 6.13 (White to move) – below – shows how one can lure the king outside the square of the pawn. With a double swap on g7, White either takes the king outside of the square of the pawn if the king recaptures the rook because of the subsequent queen swap on d7 (Qd7+) or gets a cute mate on d8 when the Black queen recaptures on g7. Work this example out by setting it up on a board so that you can explore the important tactical finesses. Diag. 6.14 shows the knight's helplessness again rook pawns. Regardless of who moves first, Black wins. But, if Black does not have the g-pawn, as in Diag. 6.15, White can win if he moves first. Note the importance of the g-pawn in Diag. 6.14.

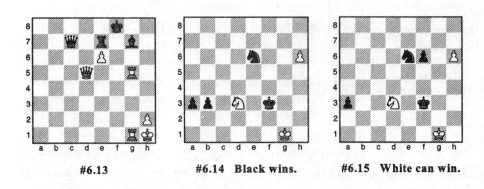

#6.13   #6.14 Black wins.   #6.15 White can win.

Two endgame guidelines should be remembered when pawn endings result: (1) push passed pawns as soon as possible and as far as feasible; and (2) push the candidate pawn (a pawn which is unobstructed by an opposing pawn) first.

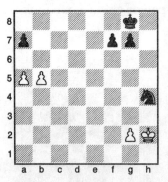

#6.16 The knight handicapped.

The strength of the pawn can be seen from looking at Diag. 6.16. White easily wins regardless of who moves first. There are two points that the diagram illustrates, however. One is that the Knight can close in on pawns very fast. If the knight was one file closer (i.e., on g5), then he could reach the pawns in time to obstruct their queening attempts. The other point is that the knight has the most problems against rook pawns because he can't maneuver on both sides of the pawn. (Remember Diag. 6.14, above?)

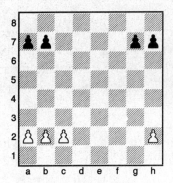

#6.17 Fewer is quicker.

The principle of advancing the candidate pawn – the pawn that is unopposed by an enemy pawn on its file – bears repeating. Another principle of pawn promotion that also needs expounding on is that it is faster to create a passed pawn when fewer pawns are opposing it. Diagram 6.17 illustrates both of these themes. In Diag. 6.17, if White does not observe the idea of advancing candidate pawns first and rashly plays his pawn to b4, then Black can advance his pawn to b5 and paralyze the White queenside pawns. As for speed, Black can create a passed pawn by playing g5 in as few as 7 moves. Whereas White would require 10 moves to create a passer on the queenside.

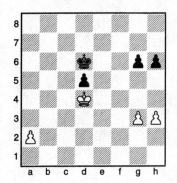

#6.18 The a-pawn wins easily.

Diagram 6.18 shows one of the strongest forces in the endgame: the outside passed pawn. It is very strong because the opposing pieces must go further to catch it, allowing the enemy king to mop up the undefended pawns on the other side of the board. From the diagram, note that the Black king will eventually have to give up protection of its pawn to chase after the passer. This allows White to kill Black's passed pawn and then attack the undefended kingside pawns.

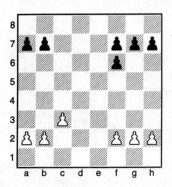

#6.19 Doubled pawns act as single pawns.

Diagram 6.19 shows a simplified position from the first game that I won against an expert. Black is lost because his kingside pawns are doubled. In positions of this sort, the pawn in front of the stacked pawns should be advanced first by White. Generally, Black's pawns will stay stacked if you allow Black to capture first on the kingside. You don't want to relieve him of his disadvantage by initiating an exchange. Also, White should not carelessly advance his kingside pawns because they may afford Black an opportunity to undouble his pawns.

85

The Opposition

Of course, queening a pawn is generally a little tougher against stronger competition. Then it will require some technique on your part before you can promote a pawn. The most important technique to know is called taking the opposition (opposing your opponent's king and forcing it to move to undesirable squares).

All single pawn endgames can potentially transform into one of the two pawn endgames below. Diag. 6.20 represents a winning position for White, regardless of who moves (assuming no mistakes, of course). For details of

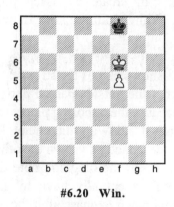

#6.20 Win.

#6.21 Draw.

how this endgame is likely to play out, see the discussion on the following page. Continuing, Diag. 6.21 represents a draw for Black, regardless of who moves first. Whether the ultimate endgame position of king-and-pawn versus king is a draw or a win depends on whether the King or the pawn occupies the 6th rank. I will consistently play the positions from the e-file; symmetrical play on the non-rook files give the same results.

#6.22 Whose on the move?

In Diag. 6.20, White wins simply because he is so close to the queening square, and Black has no backward moves to use to regain the opposition (forcing the opponent to move). For if it was White to move and the position was moved up the board one rank (Diag. 6.22), then the Black could draw – if it was White to move! In other words, with Black having the opposition (White forced to move), Black draws Diag. 6.22; if Black must move first in Diag. 6.22, White should win. **Possession of the opposition is critical**.

With White to move in Diag. 6.20 of the previous page: **1. Ke6 Ke8** (Else White plays next to e7, controlling the queening square.); **2. f6** (White takes the opposition! Black's king must move first in the face-off.) **2... Kf8; 3. f7 Kg7; 4. Ke7** and queens. With Black to move first (White having the opposition): **1... Ke8; 2. Kg7** taking control of the queening square, with f6-f7-f8-queen to follow.

With White to move in Diag. 6.21 (refer to the diagram of the previous page): **1. Ke6 Ke8** (Black takes the opposition.); **2. f7+ Kf8; 3. Kf6 stalemate**. With Black to move he must play to take the opposition whenever it is possible for the kings to face-off. See Diag. 6.23 below. This is the position that Black has to keep in mind. He wants to have the opposition from Diag. 21, forcing White to move. Otherwise, Black loses as from Diag. 6.20. So Black **plays 1... Kf7!** Now when White moves to either g5 or e5 Black must move in such a manner as to take the opposition in a king face-off. After **2. Ke5** we need a diagram: Diag. 6.24. Now **2... Kf8!** (Playing to regain the opposition!); **3. Ke6 Ke8** (Black has the opposition and will draw.); **4. f7+ Kf8; 5. Kf6 stalemate**.

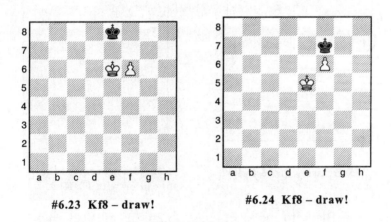

#6.23 Kf8 – draw!   #6.24 Kf8 – draw!

Let's examine Diag. 6.22 of the previous page and see if we can determine why Black is able to draw this position if he has the opposition but yet can not draw the rather similar Diag. 6.20. With Black to move in Diag. 6.22 we get: **1... Ke7; 2. Kg6!** (threatening to park the king on f6, setting up Diag. 6.20, or take control of the queening square with Kg7); **2... Kf8; 3. Kf6!** achieving Diag. 6.20 with an extra tempo and queening in five more moves. If Black has the opposition in Diag. 22, White must move: **1. Ke5 Ke7** (Maintaining the opposition.); **2. f5 Kf7!** (Any other move will allow White to set up the winning Diag. 6.20 with 3. Kf6.); **3. f6** (Diag. 6.21) **3... Kf8; 4. Ke6 Ke8; 5. f7+ Kf8; 6. Kf6 stalemate**.

The critical move was Black's 2... Kf7. Black not only keeps White's king from taking over the f6 square but positions himself to regain the opposition with 3... Kf8. This is where the difference is: If we move the position after 2... Kf7 down one rank this will put Black's king on f8. Hence White's pawn move would force Black to have to go to g7 instead of straight back since there would not be an additional rank behind him. Hence because Black has an extra rank in Diag. 6.22 on which to retreat, he can draw if he starts the position having the opposition. With this fact in mind, we can go a step further and state that even if the pawn is on its original square (which means it has a first move option of 1- or 2-move(s)), Black can keep the opposition if he starts out with it. Hence with White forced to move in Diag. 6.25 below, Black draws. Play it out – maintaining the opposition.

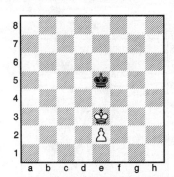

#6.25 Drawn with best play.

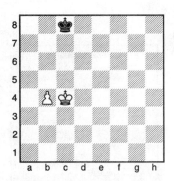

#6.26   Black recovers the opposition with 1... Kb8.

Similarly, with Black to move in Diag. 6.26, he still can draw by simply playing to recover the opposition: **1... Kb8!**. If White responds **2. Kb5, 2... Kb7** gives us a version of Diag. 6.22 where Black has the opposition. If White tries **2. Kc5**, Black counters with **2... Kc7**, taking the opposition. If **2. b5**, then **2... Kb7** gives us play similar to Diag. 6.21. And if White temporizes and plays , say, **2. Kd5**, Black grabs the **diagonal opposition** with **2... Kb7**.

There are two other observations to be made concerning Diag. 6.26. First, note that we said that Black was playing to *recover* the opposition. Second, Black's initial move to b8 was declared to be excellent. In fact, had Black moved to *any* other square he would have lost the game because it would have enabled White to assume the opposition! As well as demonstrating that the opposition can be regained (if a pawn interferes with the other player's natural moves), the diagram introduces the concept of the **distant opposition**.

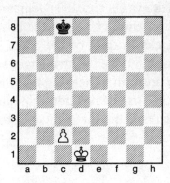

#6.27 **Black may draw.**

The key element in obtaining the opposition is to have an odd number of spaces between the kings. (Note that in the positions shown so far, the kings were separated by one space.) Whoever is first to establish this odd number (1, 3, or 5 spaces) possesses the opposition. To powerfully illustrate the usefulness of mastering the concept of the opposition, Dia. 6.27 presents a common situation where a knowledge of this technique will allow Black to draw this endgame or White to win it, depending on who moves first.

From Diag. 6.27 if White moves: **1. Kd2 Kb7** (if 1... Kd7, White captures the distant opposition with 2. Kd3, putting the odd number of 3 squares between the kings); **2.Kc3 Ka6; 3.Kc4** (White assumes the **diagonal opposition**, Diag.

#6.28 **White has the diagonal opposition.**

6.28) **Kb6; 4.Kd5 Kb7; 5.Kc5** and obviously White will win since he has two tempi to spend with pawn moves. With Black to move, he can draw with: **1... Kc7!** (Kb7 or Kd7 also draws); **2. Kd2 Kc6** (ready to take the direct opposition if White moves his king to either c3 or d3); **3. Ke3 Kc5** (taking the diagonal opposition);**4. Kd3 Kd5** (now direct opposition); **5. c3 Kc5; 6. c4 Kc6; 7. Kd4 Kd6** and draws. Demonstrate that if Black plays 1... Kd8 then 2. Kd2 (taking the distant opposition) wins for White.

Being knowledgeable of the concept of assuming the opposition is necessary for both defense and offense!

89

Common Endgame Draws

Many draws result when the endgame is reduced to a queening race and it is important to be acquainted with these so that you can avoid them or steer for them, depending upon your perspective. There are six common endgames that every chess player should know. They occur very frequently in tournaments and should be recognizable to any tournament chess player. Diagram 6.29 shows why rook pawns are the worst pawns to have in a king versus king endgame. About 90% of these occurrences end in draws because of stalemate! Diagram 6.30 shows Black achieving an easy draw through use of the rook pawn. When White checks Black he simply ducks in front of the pawn – aiming for stalemate or threatening to queen, himself, on the following move. White never gets a chance to bring his king into position to help capture the pawn. Diagram 6.31 is very similar to Diag. 6.30. In this position if White gives check at g3, Black simply runs to h1 and dares White to take the pawn and stalemate him!

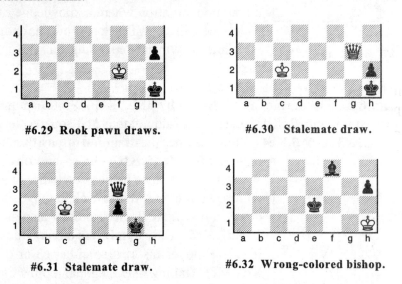

#6.29 Rook pawn draws.

#6.30 Stalemate draw.

#6.31 Stalemate draw.

#6.32 Wrong-colored bishop.

Diagram 6.32, above, is also critical to know. Black cannot queen the pawn because his Bishop does not control the queening square. Hence he can't chase the White king from the corner because his bishop is of the wrong color. The relevance of these theoretical draws can be illustrated by examining how a knowledgeable player can try to engineer them in over-the-board play. Using Diag. 6.32 as a reference, Black puts the elements together to actualize this position from Diag. 6.33. Black perceptively plays 1... Re1+; 2. Rf1 Rxf1+; 3. Kxf1 Bh3! Black has forcibly reproduced a position that is similar to Diag. 6.32. If White captures the bishop, Black simply saunters to h8 and claims the draw. On other moves Black just captures the g-pawn, himself, leaving White with an impotent h-pawn. It pays to be familiar with these common draws.

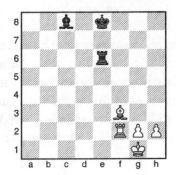

#6.33 Black makes a draw.

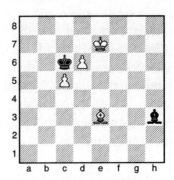

#6.34 Black sets a white-square blockade.

Diagram 6.34 (above) presents another example of the problems that can arise with opposite-colored bishops. This case of opposite-colored bishops shows why you should try to avoid them if you need to win – your bishop controls only one set of colors. Since White has no control of the white squares, Black simply marks time by moving his king or bishop, and White can make no progress. Diagram 6.35 shows another well-known draw. It is called the "merry-go-round." When White attacks the knight, it simply jumps to the other side – while staying in position to sacrifice itself for the pawn if it tries to queen. (Note also how the White king dominates the Black knight.) You simply must know these common endgames.

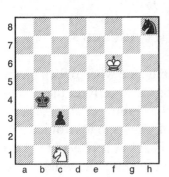

#6.35 The knight dances around the queening square.

91

Optional Skill Evaluation

COACHES: To determine how well your students have assimilated these endgame concepts and advanced in chess, a test of their technique and skill is provided as *Endgame Evaluation* in the Appendix. The eighteen positions presented measure a range of endgame skills and represent the type of material that a very capable scholastic player should be able to demonstrate.

The test has been presented to club players with USCF ratings between 1200 and 1650. (See the Appendix for information on chess ratings.) A few 1200's were able to work all of the problems except the one dealing with Philidor's Position (detailed later), while 1500-level players generally work them all – if they don't rush. So if a player is able to work most of them, you can consider the player's endgame skills to be at the 1400-level or better. Though the problems are simple, they are not trivial and hence will require some time to solve.

The test is divided into pertinent topics so that one can test the student on a respective area after they have finished studying it in the manual. Though the material on use of rooks has not been covered in depth because it includes slightly advanced topics which seem inappropriate to explain when students are still overlooking one-movers, an alert student can easily discover the proper technique through use of candidate moves.

In fact, all of the positions have a teaching aspect to them. They were chosen with care to provide a measure of the player's ability as well as to impart additional instruction.

Advancing in Chess: Basic Pawn & Rook Endgames

The weaker side can often obtain draw in a rook endgame when only a pawn down. But students need to know the positions that afford them this opportunity. The most famous of these positions is the Philidor Position, Diag. 6.36, next page, which was methodized hundreds of years ago to avoid Diag. 6.37, a winning position for White. The Philidor Position is played to force White to occupy the sixth (or third, depending on direction) rank with a pawn instead of his king. If the king is able to occupy the sixth rank first, then Diag. 6.36 arises, giving White the possibility of mate threats and practically ensuring

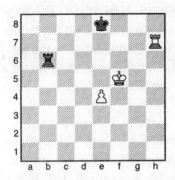

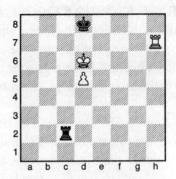

#6.36 Philidor's Position –
theoretical draw.

#6.37 Position to avoid (win).

the win. Though the draw is easier to obtain if one is familiar with these two diagrams, it can be achieved by more tortuous and error-prone methods.

The factors that the pawn-deficient side must aim for to best secure a draw are:

(1)   Try to be in a position to double attack the advancing pawn with King and Rook.
(2)   Strive to keep your king within two moves of the advancing pawn.
(3)   Play to place your king directly in front of the pawn (like Diag. 6.34) while avoiding Diag. 6.35.
(4)   As always, the defending rook is best placed behind the pawn.
(5)   Keep the rook in a position to either retard the opposing king's advance or actively check it from a distance.
(6)   Play the rook to the "long side" of the pawn so that you can obtain maximum maneuverability for your rook.

Tips for the attacker include placing the rook to cut off the defending king or provide a shield from checks from the defending rook. The attacking king is generally best placed in front of the pawn or at least nearby.

From Diag. 6.36 play could proceed: **1. e5 Ra6; 2. e6 Ra1; 3. Kf6 Rf1+** . After having first assured that the pawn occupies the sixth rank, the rook posts itself behind the pawn or gives check as convenient. From Diag. 6.37 the win comes quickly: **1 ... Kc8** (playing to the "short" side so that the rook can have

93

the longer side to maneuver – the rook needs at least three files to enable a draw); **2. Rh8+ Kb7; 3. Kd7 Rg2; 4. d6 Rg7+; 5. Ke6 Rg6+; 6. Ke7 Rg7+; 7. Kf6! Rd7; 8. Ke6 Rg7; 9. d7** and wins. (Demonstrate that if the White rook had been on g8 instead of h8, then the Black rook could played to the h-file and subsequently checked from a greater distance, enabling it to maintain a safe checking distance and draw.) The range of the defense matters.

Consider Diag. 6.38. It shows that Black can draw without using Philidor's Position and demonstrates what is meant by being on the "long side" of the pawn. Play could continue from this favorable position for White: **1. e5 Ra1**

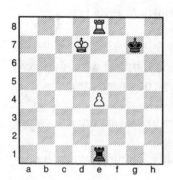

#6.38 Alternative draw.

(preparing to check horizontally); **2. Rc8 Ra7+; 3. Rc7 Ra8; 4. e6 Kf6** (closing in with the King at first opportunity); **5. Rb7 Kg7** (note that Black could not move his rook favorably); **6. Ke7 Ra1; 7. Rd7 Ra8; 8. Kd6+ Kf8; 9. e7+ Ke8; 10. Ke6 Ra6+; 11. Rd6 Ra8; 12. Rb6 Rc8** and Black draws because he has another file onto which he can move his rook. Diagram 6.39 represents a similar position with the Black rook on the "short side" of the pawn. Note that the defender must give up his drawing position if it is White to move: **1. Kf6 Kd7; 2. Kf7** and wins. Note, too, that if it was Black to move, 1... Rg6+ would force the draw.

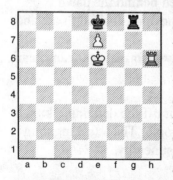

#6.39 Rook on "short" side.

Diagram 6.40 of the next page displays the other essential to know rook-pawn ending. It is called the Lucena Position after the composer who introduced it as a winning maneuver in 1497. It is not the only way to win this position (White can play Ra4-a8-d8 with the idea of using his rook or the defending king as a shield against checks) but, like the Philidor Position, it is the easiest to remember. The technique is also called "building a bridge," a more descriptive name. To win this position White could play: **1. Rc4** (If 1. Rc8+ Kd7; 2. Rc7+ Kd8 and White has made no progress. But 1. Rd2+ works as in the game.) **Ra2** (if 1... Rd1, then 2. Ra4 shields); **2. Rd4+ Ke7; 3. Kc7 Rc2+; 4. Kb6 Rb2+; 5. Kc6 Rc2+; 6. Kb5!** (the key move) **Rb2+** (If 6...

94

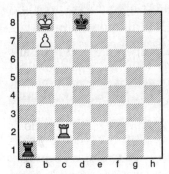

#6.40 The Lucena Position.
White to build a bridge to win.

Ke8, 7. Rd5 or if 6... Ke6, 7. Rd6+.); **7. Rb4** shielding the king from check and providing a safe bridge to the 8th rank for the pawn to shelter under while queening.

This is but an introduction to these most common endings. With the Philidor and Lucena positions as part of your technique and the guidelines given earlier, you should be able to figure out most new positions over the board.

Book Recommendations

Want to improve your endgame skills but are afraid of Rueben Fine's 571-page comprehensive tome on the endgame (*Basic Chess Endings* – recommended only for the purist or sadistic)? Then read the below recommended books.

Pandolfini's Endgame Course, Bruce Pandolfini, Simon & Schuster, NY, 1988. A collection of 239 insightful chess endings which cover the range of the most common endings. Each page presents a diagram with clear, explanatory text. The book makes an excellent companion for any young chess player needing endgame knowledge and a presentation that is easy to digest.

Silman's Complete Endgame Course, Jeremy Silman, Siles Press, Los Angeles, CA, 2007. Silman's excellent book introduces a new method of teaching the endgame, offering instruction that's tailored to fit a player's individual rating group. He stresses that "chess students need to be told which endgames are important for their particular level." This will encourage them to master a finite amount of digestible material and give them confidence to continue to develop their endgame skills as their strength and understanding grows. The book has material for the beginner and the master.

From the Middlegame Into the Endgame, Edmar Mednis, Pergamon Press, Oxford England, 1987. Transitioning to the endgame can be tricky – especially if you don't recognize that you are in an endgame! This essential book helps one to identify what an endgame is and expounds on the main principles of endgame play, offering excellent and well-thought out examples which generally cover three or more pages each. Steering your game to the ending with careful material exchanges and change of pace and attitude is emphasized.

Practical Endgame Lessons, Edmar Mednis, Batsford, UK, 1979. This is another choice book of good endgame play annotated by the once-premier writer for making endgame skills accessible. The books presents the guidelines of the endgame (move slowly, rooks behind passed pawns, give up material only to activate rooks, don't play prettily, don't prematurely exchange pieces, etc.) and shows you how to develop good "technique." Its examples are drawn from practical positions that you are likely to encounter in tournament play.

A Guide to Chess Endings, Dr. Max Euwe and David Hooper, Dover Publications, NY, 1976. This ~250-page book covers all of the endgames that you will likely ever meet over the board. Its intent is to make "a fairly thorough study of those endings most likely to occur in play, especially those with rooks." Essential endings are presented and explained in layman's terms. Anyone rated above 1100 can benefit from this book.

639 Essential Endgame Positions, Eric Schiller, Cardoza Publishing, NY, NY, 2000. Of the thousands of endgames that successful tournament players should understand, Schiller's works tries to emphasize and explain essential endgames that you need to learn. He shows how you can apply general principles and knowledge of a few hundred basic positions to more complex positions. His explanations are clear and useful for the 1400+ player – and coaches, of course!

100 Endgames You Must Know, Jesus de la Villa, News in Chess, Alkmarr, The Netherlands, 2008. The author tries to "summarize the most useful positions among the numerous endings, and to reduce them to a figure and volume that could be handled by a practical player as well as trainers or coaches." The endings targeted for examination are those that are frequently encountered in practice, those capable of being easily analyzed, and those that contain ideas that can be applied to similar and more complex positions. His selection of endgames is great and his presentation makes the ideas easy to understand and retain for practical play.

Be sure to use internet resources to help master endgame skills. Some sites have interactive endgame exercises, such as **Chess Tempo** (chesstempo.com)!

96

VIII. Team Play: A Coach's Manual

Qualification for Team Play

The majority of scholastic chess players simply want to play chess as a socializing, game-playing activity. This is fine! Chess will still add dimension to their overall thinking and scholastic development. But for those who wish to represent the school or club, a little more rigor and performance is necessary. Moreover, it is appropriate to have qualification standards simply because you might have over 50 players at your school but only 12 positions on the team.

Designated Board (or Ordered Board) Team tournaments are those team tournaments where schools are required to declare their players and assign them to a board placement. In most states, there are four players per team with two positions for alternative players (Alternates). However, some competitions allow for the formation of both an A and a B team. The A Team is regarded as the championship team and the B Team is regarded as the secondary team, consisting of members who are gaining experience to represent on the A team next year or equally-skilled players who simply could not be on the A Team because there are only 4 places available. (Georgia allows B Teams to actually compete for state titles; so be aware of your state's policy regarding B Teams.) The B Team can also have two positions for Alternates. Hence, 12 total positions are generally available.

Alternates are players who you list as part of your team so that their United States Chess Federation (USCF) and grade qualification can be established in case they have to substitute for one of your designated board players. These substitutions may be necessary because a player gets sick, is having a bad day, may need disciplining, does not show up for a round, or simply does not wish to play any longer. Substitutions may also be planned in advance to allow all six players to get an opportunity to play. For example, the coach may plan to switch Boards 3 and 4 with Alternates 1 and 2 every other round.

Again, be aware of your state's policy. Some only allow only one Alternate, and this Alternate must be the lowest rated player. More significantly, some states, such as Kentucky, will not allow Alternates to be repeatedly substituted. Once they are placed on a board, they must remain there.

97

While on the subject of coaches manipulating teams, it has been a practice of some coaches to put their best player on Board 2 (in tournaments where ratings don't set board order). This is so that their best player will not lose a point to some other competing school whose Board 1 is either feared – or known – to be better than their Board 1 player. So they reason that they will simply not risk a point. In fact, some go to the extreme of putting their weakest player on Board 1, banking on their other three players cashing in with 3 points and winning the match! This strategy backfires just as often as it succeeds. One reason for this is that some other teams may be employing the same tactics!

What the coach really needs to consider here is the team morale and perhaps even ethics. Does the number one player resent being put on Board 2? Does the number four player (by rating) resent being considered expendable and a likely loser? What is the competition really about: winning at all costs or testing one team against another to challenge both to strive for excellence? Is this manipulation – though legal – sending the wrong message to the impressionable scholastic players? And one strong caution to keep in mind is that once you submit your board order, you have locked the players in that place for the tournament! Do you really want your best player on Board 3?

Many states relieve you of the worry – if not unfairness – of manipulating teams by simply requiring that the Board order of the players reflect their rating.

Now, **how do you choose who will represent the school or club?** There are many basis for consideration: classroom attendance or participation, tournament performance, experience and rating, and perhaps even subjective expectation. Best for objective qualification based on skill level and performance is (1) a series of qualifying chess tournaments or (2) using a club ladder established by rated games.

The use of a club challenge ladder to establish the relative strength of your chess players is a recognized method. The listing of chess players by rating (and, hopefully, skill level) allows the players to prove themselves, determine their skill level (and perhaps USCF rating group), and to identify worthy opponents. One has to be especially cautious with the latter point because most fair players will want to challenge the top players almost constantly.

Too, you will find some players who will want only to play their favorite victim and accumulate points.

The way to handle this is to allow challenge of your top players only by the better players. In other words, one must be able to compete with better players before they can challenge the best. The tournament director can simply state that players must be within, say, 300 points to challenge each other. As for playing victims constantly, simply limit consecutive games with the same opponent to less than three straight and encourage play of different opponents by awarding bonus points for number of games and play against a variety of players at different rating levels. Most importantly, insist that all USCF rules be observed during challenge matches: no talking, touch-move, recording moves, and clock use (if available).

A simple listing of players in their relative strength order can be okay. What is best, though, is to establish a rated listing. You may adopt the USCF rating structure or simply form your own simplified system to quickly rank players. (See *How to Calculate Ratings* of the Appendix for a simplification of the USCF's algorithm.) The level at which you set your base rating does not matter much. Once your players begin to compete in USCF-rated tournaments, you will be able to see how your school or club ratings correspond to actual USCF-rated performance. The main thing is to simply establish a system and consistently use it. You can encourage participation by awarding medals, trophies, ribbons, or certificates at the end of the school year based on the rating improvement of each player or simply recognize the highest achievers of a rating class. While handing out awards, be sure to reserve awards for players who (1) consistently record their games best, (2) have excellent classroom deportment, and (3) take assignments seriously.

A suggested club rating system for players who don't have established USCF ratings can be organized as the following suggestions obtained from the *A Guide to Scholastic Chess* at the USCF website (www.uschess.org):

- *If you are just starting at the beginning of the year, and no one has a club rating, everyone starts at 900 points.*

- *In your first school tournament, a player receives 15 points for every win and loses 15 points for every loss.*

- *In future tournaments, higher-rated players receive 10 points for every win in their section and lose 15 points for every loss. Lower-rated players receive 15 points for every win against a higher-rated player in their section, but only lose 5 points for a loss.*

- *In the case of draws or stalemates, the higher-rated player loses 10 points and the lower-rated player gains 10 points.*

- *When a tournament ends, bonus points can be awarded to the top three players in each section. The first place finisher could receive 25 points, second place 15, and third place 10. Bonus points are usually awarded in the first few months of the chess club year, to help players find their level more quickly.*

EXAMPLE: Jim is rated 1250 and loses a game to Bill, who is rated 1100. To calculate the new rating, subtract 15 points from Jim's club rating (because he was the higher-rated player and he lost). Bill receives 15 points (he was the lower-rated player and he won). Therefore, Jim's new club rating is 1235 and Bill's new club rating is 1115.

This is a very simple system that takes little time to calculate new ratings for the students. Consider giving bonus points for games won at a local tournament. This rewards them for their participation. However, restrict points to no more than 10 points per won game. Never subtract points for losses.

A variation of this is to let all players start at 900 as before, but for each game won add 25 points plus or minus 10% of the difference in ratings, with a maximum of 50 points.

Qualifying chess tournaments can be a reasonable basis of identifying your chess team members. Because everyone does not play each other in these tournaments, you might not get a good idea how your better chess players rank with other top players. The good point of tournament competition is that it does demonstrate how well the players conduct themselves under tournament conditions. In fact, you might find that this method is superior to determining placement by a challenge-ladder placement. The bad point of these tournaments is that some of your good players might not be available for a particular tournament and so you lose a valuable data point – especially if you use less than three qualifying tournaments to determine placement.

What such qualifying tournaments can do is to help you narrow down a large group of players into some smaller, team-candidate group which can then be played as a round robin tournament, where every contestant plays each other. Moreover, if you think someone is particularly worthy even if he had a sub-par result in the qualifying tournament, you can simply seed him into the round robin based on past performance or perhaps team experience. Meriting a position based upon a round robin result allows few doubts or speculation.

The qualifying chess tournaments don't actually have to be events that you coordinate. Individual participation in local scholastic tournaments can give you a good basis to judge the candidate's performance and desire to play. Too, you could even use local scholastic tournament participation as a requirement or bonus consideration to any school-organized qualifying tournaments. Keep in mind that those who compete in individual scholastic tournaments have tournament experience and their parents both approve and support their tournament play. It does not matter that Johnny is the best player if his parents won't allow his participation on the team or if Johnny – God forbid! – does not want to play in team competition.

Your best method for determining team qualification and placement is to combine a rating ladder with tournament performance and knowledge mastery.

Mastery of essential chess knowledge is probably the best way of determining who will be part of the team – as long as they have the competitive bent for tournament chess and play consistently at their skill level. As stated earlier, this book is based on the premise that there is specific knowledge that all fair scholastic chess players are familiar with and those who aspire to represent the school or club should be expected to be able to demonstrate this knowledge. Therefore a listing of the elements that the players need to have mastered if they plan to represent the school or club are listed below with the reference section in which the information is contained. Observation of the student's games and other tests can be used to test whether or not they have mastered the material. It is not sufficient that they have been exposed to the information – you should expect them to be able to demonstrate it, preferably under tournament conditions.

The following items must be mastered before one will be considered to be eligible to represent in tournament competition:

- Know the point value of all the chess pieces. [Sect. 1, **p. 1**]

- Know what the Scholars' Mate is and how to avoid it when playing Black. [Sect. 2, **pp. 25-31**]

- Know how to promote a pawn to a queen or other piece. [Sect. I, **p. 4**; Sect. VI, **pp. 81-85**]

- Know what the opposition is and how to use it for pawn promotion [Sect. VI, **pp. 86-89**]
- Know what taking a pawn *en-passant* (in passing) means. [Sect. I, **pp. 5**]

- Know how to keep score. [Sect. 1, **pp. 7-10**; Sect. VII, **p. 107–108**]

- Demonstrate good opening play, developing pieces and castling early. [Sect. II, **pp. 17-22**]

- Know the king-rook mate and be able to execute it within 40 moves. [Sect. III, **pp. 41-43**]

- Know the difference between stalemate and checkmate.[Sect. III, **p. 47-48**]

- Know what the 50-move drawing rule means. [Sect. III, **pp. 46-47 & 50**]

- Know what a draw by three-fold repetition of position means. [Sect. III, **p. 46 & 49**]

- Know what a draw by insufficient mating chances means. [Sect. III, **p. 46 &49**; Sect. VII, **p. 105–106**]

102

- Know where rooks belong to either promote one's own or stop the opponent's pawns.   [Sect. VI, **pp. 82-83**]

- Be familiar enough with a chess clock so that its use does not distract from one's play.   [Sect. VII, **pp. 103-104**]

- Play touch-move chess.   [Sect. VII, **p. 108**]

- Keep quiet while chess games are ongoing – yours or others. [Sect. VII, **p. 104–105**]

Rules and Conduct

The following rules are included here to answer frequently asked questions and to remind players of useful information. They are not intended to supersede or modify anything in the USCF *Official Rules of Chess*. In fact, one should refer to the most recent USCF rulings to assure that these rules have not been modified! The rules and conduct of team play are similar to those for individual play except for the stipulation which allows a team captain to guide a player in their decision on whether or not to accept a draw. To comply with users' requests, the topics are listed alphabetically rather than grouped by subject or pertinence.

Analysis of Games. Do not analyze your games in the tournament room. Analyze your games outside.

Check. Announcing check is not required. It is the responsibility of the opponent to notice the check, and a player who does not may suffer serious consequences (See the touch-move rule).

Clocks and Time Controls. Players have a specified time in which the game must be completed (Sudden Death Time Control) or a certain amount of moves must be completed. (For example, 40 moves in 2 hours is a popular time limit for standard tournaments.) In scholastic play, most games have a time control of an hour or less *per side*. This means that you and your opponent may each have an hour on your clock, amounting to a two-hour game. If you have an hour time control, initially set your clock at 5:00. Then each player must complete the entire game before the flag falls at 6:00. If one's flag fall before the game is completed, they forfeit the game on time.

Clocks with move counters and flag fall indicators are legal. However, it is the USCF policy that move counters should not be relied upon, and in case of a time forfeiture claim only the score sheets of the players may be used to validate or repudiate the claim.

Clocks must remain running at all times, except when a tournament director (TD) is being summoned by either player to resolve a dispute. A player who wishes to make a claim of any sort or to see a TD for any legitimate reason may stop both clocks and raise his hand to summon a TD. If a clock is not available at the start of a game, the players must begin without one. If a clock later becomes available during the game, call a TD and he will set the clock for you. Except when stopping their clock upon completion of their move, or stopping both clocks while summoning a TD, players are not permitted to touch a clock while the game is in progress.

Generally, the player of the black pieces has the choice of which players' clock will be used. Moreover, a digital clock with time-delay capability is preferable to any other clock in a game with any Sudden Death time control. Therefore, if White has such a clock available and Black does not, White's clock should be used. The only occasions in which Black retains the right to use his clock are in games with no Sudden Death time control, in cases where both players have the same type of clock, or if White is late and Black has already set up his equipment (as long as Black's equipment is standard).

If a digital clock is used in a tournament that has a 60 min./Game format, the time delay should be set at 5 seconds per move with the base time control of 60 minutes. (Some tournaments may modify this and stipulate that 5 minutes be deducted to compensate for the additional seconds per move.) Because the use of time delay presumes that a person will be have an increment of time to complete any move, many claims of insufficient losing chances will be resolved by allowing the player to demonstrate his ability to neutralize the threats of his opponent.

Conduct of Players. Try to keep as quiet as possible on the tournament floor so that other players are not disturbed. You may not speak to anyone while your game is in progress unless a TD is present. If there is a problem of any kind during your game, alert a TD immediately. If you wait until after your game is over, the TD will probably be unable to change the result, even if your claim was correct. You may not consult any chess books, computers or other material during the game. If you leave the tournament room during your game, such as to go to the bathroom, you should not speak with anyone. If you believe that your opponent is trying to distract or intimidate you, alert a TD immediately. Even though a TD may be witnessing some apparently obnoxious behavior, he may not correct the situation until the opponent complains that the actions are disturbing.

Draws. If you want to offer a draw to your opponent, you should do so after you make a move but before you start your opponent's clock. Your opponent may decline the draw offer by saying so or by moving a piece. A draw offer is valid until it is rejected by the opponent. If both players agree to a draw, the game is over. A reasonably complete and accurate scoresheet is required to claim a draw by triple occurrence of position or under the 50-move rule. If such a claim is found to be incorrect, two minutes will be added to the opponent of the claimant's remaining time.

<u>Coordinated Draw Offers</u>. Draw offers made as a member of a team can be coordinated through the team captain. A player is allowed to ask the team captain whether a draw is acceptable based upon the team standings. The captain must respond to this inquiry by looking only at the Team Results record. He should not look at or comment on the player's game position, offer coaching, or base his decision upon the player's ability to win. His decision should be based solely upon whether a half-point is desirable from a team standpoint. The decision to accept or reject the draw offer is still solely that of the player. For more on this important subject from a team standpoint, see *Duties of the Team Captain.*

<u>Sudden Death Rules.</u> *Upon request of a player* a tournament director (TD) may rule that the game is drawn if the position is clearly drawn, if the player has insufficient losing chances, or if neither player is making progress. To make such a request, a player should stop both clocks and call a TD to rule on the claim.

A claim of a draw based on insufficient losing chances will be upheld if the TD believes that a Class C player would have little chance to lose the position against a Master if both had ample time. Such a claim can only be made by a player with less than five minutes remaining on his clock. If the TD believes that the claim is clearly incorrect, one minute will be subtracted from the claimant's remaining time. If the TD is uncertain regarding the validity of the claim, the TD may temporarily deny it, make no time adjustment, and watch the game with the intent of awarding the draw if the opponent is making no progress. The TD may also invite a later re-claim if the opponent is making no progress.

As an alternative the TD may, at his discretion, place a digital clock with time-delay capability on the game. If such a clock is placed on the game, the claimant gets half of his remaining time, up to but not exceeding one minute, and the opponent's time is not adjusted. The time delay is set for five seconds, and the game continues until a result is achieved.

Claiming insufficient losing chances is also considered a draw offer. It is the same as any other draw offer: good for that move only. If the opponent chooses to play on he may win, lose, or draw; but cannot say a few moves later, "I'll take that draw now." He may offer another draw later, of course, but the draw offer of the original claim is no longer valid.

Another very important sudden-death ruling is that a player may claim **a time forfeit in sudden death** only if he stops the clock before both flags fall. If both flags are down, the game is drawn upon the claim of either player or upon a ruling by the TD under USCF Rule 14G2.

Illegal Moves. If it is discovered that one of either player's last ten moves was illegal, the position will be reinstated to what it was before the illegal move, and the game shall continue by applying the touch-move rule to the move replacing the illegal move. Clocks will not be reset.

In a sudden death time control two minutes will be added to the remaining time of the opponent of the player who made the illegal move. If either player has less then five minutes remaining and the illegal move is not corrected before the opponent of the player who made the illegal move completes two moves, the illegal move stands and there is no time adjustment.

A player must call an illegal move. The TD will not call any illegal moves. Nor should spectators point out any illegal moves.

Interference. No interference in any game by spectators, other players, coaches, or parents will be tolerated. Penalties include expulsion from the tournament. Only the player involved should point out irregularities to a TD. This should be done by raising one's hand to summon a TD.

Late Arrival. A player who is more than one hour late for a round (of an hour or more duration) loses the game by forfeit and will normally be dropped from the tournament. The hour is measured from the actual starting time of the round which may not be the scheduled starting time. A player should start his opponent's clock once the TD announces that the round has begun. If the player with the white pieces is present and Black is absent, White can, first, start his own clock, make his move on the board, and then start Black's clock. If a clock is not available at the start of a round, any elapsed time before one becomes available will be split between both players. If both players are late for the start of a round, the first to arrive must split the elapsed time before starting the opponent's clock.

Pairings. Most scholastic tournaments will be conducted as Swiss Tournament Events, where the top half of a score group plays the bottom half. Individuals will generally be paired with other individuals who have the same score each round. Individuals should not receive the same color three times in a row unless there is no other way to pair the score group or unless necessary to equalize colors. If you believe there is a pairing error, report it to a TD immediately! Once the round starts, it will probably be too late to correct any mistakes.

Recording Moves. Each Player is strongly encouraged to record the moves. A player who chooses not to do so gives up the right to claim a draw by triple occurrence of position or the 50-move rule, and gives up the right to challenge such claims by his opponent. If a player is not keeping score, his opponent can ask a TD to require that the player do so. If the TD determines that the player knows how to keep score, then the player will be required to keep score. If such a request is refused, 5 min. may be deducted from his time. In a Sudden Death time control, neither player is obligated to keep score when either player has less than five minutes left on the clock.

Players using electronic recording devices – such as the **Monroi Scorekeeping** system – are required to move before they record their move. If you opponent is using the Monroi System, keep the following security tips in mind: (1) alert the TD if the player using the Monroi appears to be making too many moves with it or seems to be doing excessive writing; (2) assure that the player does not leave the table with the recording device; and, (3) assure that the unit is an approved USCF-sanctioned recording device.

Reporting Results. Immediately upon completion of the game the players should mark their result on the pairing sheet for their section. Both players are responsible for verifying that their result is posted correctly. In the case of team competition, players should make sure that their captains have their score. They should both assure that the correct score has been recorded on the Team Results Record.

Time Forfeits. Only a player involved in the game may claim a time forfeit. No other player, parent, coach, spectator or TD may make such a claim or bring the fall of a flag to the attention of the players. No score sheet is required to forfeit an opponent in a Sudden Death time control.

Touch-move. If you intentionally touch a piece when it is your turn to move, that piece must be moved if it can be done so legally. If you intentionally touch an enemy piece when it is your turn to move, the enemy piece must be captured if you can do so legally. You must say "I adjust" before touching a piece if you want to adjust that piece on the board. You should do so only when it is your turn. If you accidentally release a piece on an unintended but legal square, you must leave it there. If you intend to castle, you should touch your king first (though one is not penalized if the rook is first moved). Obvious accidental disturbance of the pieces will not be considered touching.

Tournament Directors (TD). Tournament Directors direct and supervise the play, assuring that rules are observed and rounds timely conducted. TDs will be on the tournament floor at all times to assist you in the event of any problem or question. Just raise your hand and keep it in the air until a TD comes to assist you. Remember that a TD will generally not interfere with your game. It is up to you to make a claim. If you think that a TD has ruled incorrectly concerning your game, you should ask to appeal to the Chief TD immediately. When summoning the TD, you may stop your clock.

Other Rules. All other rules or decisions will be based upon the *Official Rules of Chess* as published by the United States Chess Federation. Penalties for rules violations are at the discretion of the TD and may vary from warnings and time penalties to forfeitures and expulsion from the tournament.

Duties of the Team Captain

It is not necessary that the team captain be the number one board. Any actively-playing team member can be the team captain. It may even be desirable to make some other player than Board 1 the captain so as to reduce the distractions on what may be the most critical board. The Team Results Record is kept at the captain's board but in plain sight so that other players can see the standings at a glance without having to bother the captain.

The captain should:

• Make sure that all participants are seated in listed order.

• Make sure that teammates have their assigned color.

• Make sure that the team listing is properly filled out.

• Report any substitutions or withdrawals to the Pairing Room Director or TD.

• Make sure that all Alternates fill in from the bottom up. This means that if an alternative is added to replace Board 1, the previous Board 2 becomes the new Board 1, the previous Board 3 becomes the new Board 2, the previous Board 4 becomes the new Board 3, and the Alternate becomes the new Board 4. If Board 3 has to sit out because of being absent, bad play, or sickness, Board 1 and 2 stay as assigned, Board 4 becomes the new Board 3, and the Alternate becomes the new Board 4. The new Team Results Record should reflect the current participants in board order.

• Alternates should **never** be seated above any designated Boards.

• Remain aware of the team score.

- Respond to requests from teammates of whether a draw is acceptable from the team-placement standpoint. In this case, the captain can only say that a draw is okay or needed. He may also say that a win is needed to win the match. He cannot say things like: "You should be able to win that position" or "You look like you are in such bad shape that a draw would be nice." **He can only speak of what a draw would mean to the team standings without reference to the player's actual game position.** What **he definitely cannot** do is look at the player's position and comment on it! His decision must be based upon the team standings alone – not the position on the chess board. In fact, if the captain is unsure of how to respond to a player because some of the other games have not been decided, the most he can do is to say something neutral like: "I am uncertain whether a draw would help the team at this point. Look at the other game positions and decide for yourself." He could say "I would not personally take a draw at the moment because I don't know what the other scores are." He can't say: "Keep playing – your position is better" or "The worst that you can do in your game is draw from that position so don't be in a hurry to accept the draw." *The decision to accept or reject the draw offer is solely that of the player.*

- Designate a teammate to act as his replacement if he has to leave the room.

- Assure that a result is obtained for all games.

- Once the round is over, sign and submit the Team Results Record to the official tournament score keeper.

- Receive any team awards or trophies on behalf of the team. The captain may also designate this duty to others, such as a teammate or coach.

Duties of a Coach

Some of the duties of the coach overlaps those of the captain. The more responsibility that the coach undertakes, the less distraction that the captain will have. Under no circumstances can the coach comment on any position or interfere in a chess game.

- Make sure that his team and any Alternates are properly registered.

- Make sure that his team checks in to be paired for the first round. He can delegate this responsibility to a team player or sponsor, if desired.

- Make sure that all fees are paid as well as memberships secured (United States Chess Federation dues, state membership fees, tournament entry, etc.).

- Provide for the team members needs (food, rest area, telephone access, etc.) and assist with their questions, such as where to get a scoresheet or where the restrooms are.

- Assure that all team members are present at the start of the round.

- In an open Swiss format tournament, identify all players who are in attendance and assure that they are coded as part of the team.

- Advise the team of the rules, emphasizing no talking, touch-move, and calling a TD for questions.

- Stress the importance of the half-point for team scores. The individual scores comprise the team score. Each game result will add into the team score. For a four-round team match, 2.5 points out of 4 points wins the match. Hence if your team has already garnered 2 points, then it is okay for any of the remaining games to end in a draw.

- Designate a team captain.

- Advise the team members on how they should conduct themselves when inquiring of the captain whether a draw is helpful to the team, emphasizing that the captain cannot evaluate their position in making this decision.

- Assure that team members are seated in listed order.

- Provide scoresheets and equipment for the team.

- Report any substitutions or withdrawals to the Pairing Room Director or TD.

- Make sure that all Alternates fill in from the bottom up. This means that if an alternative is added to replace Board 1, the previous Board 2 becomes the new Board 1, the previous Board 3 becomes the new Board 2, the previous Board 4 becomes the new Board 3, and the Alternate becomes the new Board 4. If Board 3 has to sit out because of being absent, bad play, or sickness, Board 1 and 2 stay as assigned, Board 4 becomes the new Board 3, and the Alternate becomes the new Board 4. The new Team Results Record should reflect the current participants in board order. Remember: Alternates should **never** be seated above any designated Boards.

- If a captain has to leave the room, coordinate the designation of a substitute with him and the floor TD.

- Make sure that the Team Results sheet is properly filled out and signed.

- Submit the Team Results to the official tournament score keeper.

- Check the standings to make sure that the scores have been properly posted and are in accord with the Team Results record.

- At the conclusion of an Individual/Team tournament, designate which four players should be used to determine the team score.

- Attend the parents' and coaches' meeting for notification of rules and tournament information as well as to provide input and direction on ideas or formats that you or your school prefer.

Team Format

Many of the duties and problems of the captain as well as the coach can be avoided simply by using a different format to select teams for competition.

Hence a very popular format that is primarily used in states that have large scholastic chess populations (such as Texas and New York) is to have a combined Individual and Team event. There is no limit placed on how many players from a school participate. This has the added benefit of allowing individuals without a team to participate. Too, the players can generally sign up at the door and aren't required to pre-register. (Verify this beforehand as New Mexico and a few other states require pre-registration.) Hence many of the administrative tasks – such as having playoffs to determine board order, coordination of Alternatives' participation, submitting a Team Results Record, and burdening a player with the duties of Captain – can be circumvented with this format. In fact, in the Texas Scholastic Championship, you don't even have to officially declare a team until the competition is over!

The Individual/Team format makes it possible for everyone from a school to play. No one is barred because of skill. Too, having the team score decided by totaling the top four (or five–Oklahoma; or three–New Jersey Primary) scorers at the end can be beneficial–especially if your higher-rated players fail to rack up good scores (perhaps due to draws against other high-rated opponents) and one of your lower-rated players performs well above his rating. And, of course, having this combined format means that state organizations need to sponsor only one tournament to decide both the individual and team champions.

Georgia has a combination of team format approaches. Their High School championship is contested in the ordered board format where 5 boards constitute a team. (Their College Team Championship is run on a 4-person ordered board format.) But their Primary (K-3), Elementary (K-5), and Middle School (6-8) may utilize two different formats.

For instance, the metro Atlanta area has three regional qualifying events in which schools may send as many players as they desire. This is run on the Open Individual/Team format where the sections are paired individually with the absolute restriction that no one can play someone from their own school. (Some states soften this restriction and allow pairing of team members in the final round to better determine Individual Champions.) The top five scores for each school in each of the three sections constitute the team score. Next, the top scoring teams for each section from these three regional qualifying events then move on to the State K-8 Team Finals where they are joined by other school teams from outside the metro Atlanta region. In contrast, the State K-8 Team Finals is run on the 5-person ordered board format just like the HS Championship.

New York differs drastically from most states because they have a large number of high-rated players. Hence they don't bar teams from other states participating in the New York State Scholastic Championship tournament. Of course, the NY champion titles – based on the top four scorers from a school – will be awarded only to NY residents.

What is generally consistent across the United States is the breakdown of grades and inclusion of home schooled (or virtual schooled) students. Home schooled and private schooled students are generally delineated as follows: Primary K-3, Elementary K-5; Middle 6-8; and High School 9-12. Most states define home-schooled and virtual-schooled players similarly. A home schooled student is defined as a student who receives at least 50% of his/her core curriculum instruction at home. A virtual school student is defined as one who receives at least 50% or his/her core curriculum instruction on-line but not in the school building.

In general, states allow students attending the same school to play up into higher sections even from lower grades, but not vice-versa. If an Elementary Section is listed as K-5, most states will allow a 6th grader to play in this section if his particular school is a K-6 Elementary school. However, a sixth-grader enrolled in a Middle School cannot play down into the Elementary Section. This is similar for Middle Schools that includes grades 6-9 and High Schools that overlap with grades 9-12. (There are exceptions. For instance, the state of Washington allows a 6th grader –not a whole team of 6th graders – that attends a middle school to play down into an associated Elementary Section or represent in the Jr. High Section.) In general, if the school is *physically and administratively separate, then it is considered a separate school* and the player, consequently, loses his privilege of shifting into different sections.

Because the Individual/Team competitions are conducted as Individual tournaments, use of this format does not involve a lot of strategy or coordination, unlike the Designated Board tournaments. Since most state prohibit team members from competing against each other until the later rounds when there might be a 2-point gap between the top scorers and the next non-team member, there is not much strategy – or manipulation – involved in these events.

So it is incumbent upon you as player or coach to know what format for team competition that your state has adopted. Pre-registration will be favored by most states so that they can verify a player's school and grade and perhaps assign them a unique school code.

Team Specifics for Designated Board Play

Because I am familiar with scholastic tournaments conducted in Tennessee, I will use Tenn. as an example of the Designated Board (or Ordered Board) Team tournament.

Other states may have different policies for substitutions as well as team composition. For instance, other states have 5-player teams and only three divisions: Elementary/Primary (K-5), Middle School (K-8), and High School (K-12). Kentucky has a fifth division created by segregating first grade and below into a section. And states like New York and New Jersey have eight divisions of their scholastics, segregating players below a certain rating into Reserve Sections.

Tennessee generates four championship teams from each of its four major regions and these teams move on to comprise the Team Finals tournament. As for qualifying for the Finals, a school may have as many teams in a school division as it can field. Too, home schools have the same rights to field teams as public schools. Alternate substitution works similar in both the qualifying tournament and the Finals.

For Alternates' substitution, a survey shows that most states and the policy of the USCF is to close ranks toward the top. This concept will be explained with examples because it is the source of some confusion, and – if done improperly – could result in a team or school being disqualified.

Let us use Public Elementary School as an example, which has grades from kindergarten through sixth. First of all, Public Elementary School will have to qualify in a regional team tournament to get seeded into the State Finals. It is emphasized that it's the school that is qualified to appear in the Team Finals tournament, not the specific team which emerges in the top four from the region. A school can have an entirely different line-up than the players who represented it in the qualifying tournament. But the school can have only one championship team in each division. In this case, Public Elementary can field a Primary Team (grades K-3) and an Elementary Team (grades K-6). Note that any player can play up – though it is not recommended to place a player two divisions above his grade – but no one from a higher grade level can play in a lower division. If you have a school that has joint primary and high school level education, it is allowable to have a Jr. High player appear on the high school team. Any grouping to form a complete team is preferable to fielding a short team of two or three players.

B Teams

As stated earlier, a full team consists of four players and as many as two Alternates. (Other states, such as Pennsylvania, allows only one alternate.) Moreover, if your school has a Championship Team entered into the Finals, they can also have as many "B" Teams as they wish.

Your B Teams will likely play other schools' B Teams. They may even have to play among themselves if you send four or five teams and there are only three or so other B Teams present. This will likely happen if your teams consistently win or lose in a Swiss and you have more than three teams in a division. Moreover, your Primary B Team may play either Elementary, Jr. High, or even High School B Teams! In earlier years, an Elementary level B Team actually played among High School level B Teams and captured second place honors! It all depends upon how many B Teams show up overall. B Team players get rated games, gain experience and confidence, and assure that you have a edge in next year's competition because of the experience base that you have built. (In other states, B-Teams also qualify to win the overall championship titles, such as in Georgia.)

In fact, an excellent method to assure that your Alternates for the Championship Team get some activity so that their parents don't feel it is a waste of time to bring them to the tournament "just in case" is to list them as part of a B Team. In other words, an Alternate of your Championship Team can be listed as a board member of your B Team. Moreover, your B Teams can also have Alternates. Therefore, if your school can field enough representatives, you will always have the maximum four boards to garner points for your team. You can also have the same person listed as an Alternate of both the Championship and B Team. The Pairing Director will strive to give Alternates a game – often rated – each round against each other so that they will remain primed for play, possibly obtain a rating, and not simply be used as backup. (Not all Regions provide rated games but they do provide playing opportunities for Alternates.)

Before you get over-zealous and try fielding multiple teams, consider that at the Finals the players will have to join the USCF because the tournament is rated. (Of course participants on the Championship Team must also be USCF members.) Moreover, it is advisable that your players pay this fee before they appear at the door to register. It could upset everyone if someone balked at the reasonable fee and resulted in your team being undermanned.

Alternate Substitutions

Now to the business of substitutions, whose guidelines are similar for most states. Let us say that Public Elementary has the following board lineup for Round 1:

Round 1 Seating		
Board	Player	Color
Board 1	A	White
Board 2	B	Black
Board 3	C	White
Board 4	D	Black
1st Alternate	AA	
2nd Alternate	BB	

In Round 1, your team sits on one side of the table and plays alternating colors. (The Alternates are nearby and accessible but not seated at the playing table.) For instance, if A has White, then B will have Black and C will have White. (Coaches should assure that the Team Results Records reflect this board and color arrangement as well as the wall chart.) The Board 1 of the opposing team will then play Black against A and the Board 2 of the opposing Team will play White against B, etc.

Now let us suppose that in Round 2 you want to give your Alternates some activity or that you had to pull a player from the lineup because of sickness. For argument's sake, let's pull B from the lineup because he has a headache. In this case, A stays on Board 1, C moves to Board 2, and D moves to Board 3. Now any Alternate can be placed on Board 4. Let's choose Alternate BB instead of Alternate AA. The team has closed ranks toward the top.

Round 2 Seating		
Board	Player	Color
Board 1	A	Black
Board 2	C	White
Board 3	D	Black
Board 4	BB	White
New 2nd Alternate	AA	
Preferred Board 2	B	

Remember, there is no substitution order for Alternates when they are replacing only one board during a round. However, if both Alternates are put in during the same round, Alternate AA must be placed on a higher board than Alternate BB because precedence does matter. To help clarify this arrangement, think of the Alternates as Board 5 and 6, respectively. Your top-ranked Alternate must always precede your "Board 6" Alternate. Hence, *if Alternate BB has already been placed on a board before Alternate AA is substituted during a following round, Alternate BB simply drops to the board below Alternate AA even though he actively manned a board first.*

In Round 3, B feels better so we return him to the team. Moreover, we decide to remove C (Board 2 in Round 2 but originally Board 3) and D (Board 3 in Round 2 but originally Board 4) from the team. In this case, B returns to Board 2, Alternate BB becomes Board 4, and Alternate AA moves onto Board 3 because of his pre-determined precedence. Please note that when a player is assigned a board, he plays that board upon his return – unless he must be moved up to a higher board because the player listed ahead of him was removed for some reason. Let's see how the boards stack up now:

Round 3 Seating		
Board	Player	Color
Board 1	A	White
Board 2	B	Black
Board 3	AA	White
Board 4	BB	Black
Preferred Board 3	C	
Preferred Board 4	D	

Ready for more musical chairs? Well, let Round 4 commence with some substitutions, also. If any of the original players return to the lineup, the Alternates will drop out in order of usage. So BB will drop first because he mans the lowest board. If all the originally listed players return, they assume the boards that they were originally assigned and the Alternates simply wait out the round or play games among other Alternates. Now if it happens that one of your Alternates or any of the substituted players can't return to the lineup, you must simply play the round a player short. But what now happens if only Board 4 returns to the lineup? Well, since he was a seeded board member in the team lineup, he has preference over all Alternates and so assumes control of Board 3. Note that Alternate AA gets two consecutive Whites because of this board shift. See the following table (next page) for Round 4 seating.

119

Round 4 Seating		
Board	Player	Color
Board 1	A	Black
Board 2	B	White
Board 3	D	Black
Board 4	AA	White
New 2nd Alternate	BB	
Preferred Board 3	C	

Cardinal Rule: No Alternate player can ever be seated above an active Designated Board player.

In summation, the following points should be remembered.

1. If you have a Championship Team in a section, you can have as many B-Teams as you desire and can field. For example, if you have a Primary Championship Team (you can have only one Championship Team per division), then you can have as many Primary-level B Teams as you want. Keep in mind that your B Teams may have to play each other. They may also have to play Elementary, Jr. High, or High School Teams.

2. Alternate substitution closes ranks toward the top.

3. If Board 1 leaves for a round and returns, he must be reseated at Board 1. If a lower board leaves and returns, he will be optionally seated at his original board or moved up to the next highest board if a player on an originally-designated board higher than his is absent.

4. Alternates will play on the lowest available board. Alternate 2 can play instead of Alternate 1. Even though Alternate 2 may man a board before Alternate 1, Alternate 1 will play the higher board whenever **both** Alternates are substituted.

5. It is highly recommend that a Championship Team have at least one Alternate. In this manner you will be assured of fielding a full team each round.

6. Alternates may both represent the Championship Team and hold a board on the B Team. They may even be allowed to simultaneously play on both teams during a particular round!

7. All teams MUST check-in to be paired for the first round. A player or the team coach may perform this duty.

Glossary

Alternate. An alternative or substitute player for a team.

Bishop pair. Possession of both bishops, which cooperatively control the diagonals, amplifying their power.

Blockade. To prevent advancement of enemy pieces or pawns into your territory. Pieces are blockaded by the strategical placement of your pawns (or pieces) to exclude entry.

Castle. Another name for the rook. As a verb, it refers to castling.

Castling. Moving the king and rook simultaneously. This is the only situation where two pieces can be repositioned on the same move. To castle, move the king two squares to the right or left and place the rook on the square to the king's opposite side.

Center. The geometric center of the board encompassed by the rectangle c4-c5-f5-f4.

Checkmate. An attack against the enemy king from which he cannot escape (such as by moving away, capturing the attacking piece, or placing a piece between the attacker to block the check).

Combination. A sequence of forcing moves played to attain a specific goal, generally initiated by a sacrifice of material.

Development. The process of moving pieces from their original starting squares to new positions where they control more squares.

Discovered check. An attack uncovered when a piece moves out of the way and exposes the king to attack by the piece that shielded behind it.

Doubled pawns. Two pawns of the same color stacked up on the same file.

Draw. A tied game, which can result from a stalemate, three-time repetition of position, or mutual agreement.

En passant. A French term meaning *in passing*. It refers to the capture of a pawn which advances two squares on its first move and passes an enemy pawn on an adjacent file of the 5th rank. The enemy pawn can capture the passing pawn as if it only moved one square. This optional capture must be immediately made on the move on which it first becomes possible.

Endgame. The final stage of a chess game. It is generally reached when the queens are exchanged and there are few pieces remaining on the board.

Fianchetto. An Italian term that means *on the flank* and indicates development of bishops at either g2, b2, g7, or b7.

File. A vertical column of eight squares, i.e., a-file, b-file, etc.

Force. The material (pawns and pieces) present.

Fork. A tactical maneuver in which a piece or pawn attacks two enemy pieces or pawns simultaneously.

Initiative. The ability to make threats to which your opponent must react.

Insufficient mating material. A lack of material to enforce mate, generally referring to a position where a player has only a lone knight or bishop.

Insufficient losing chances. A drawn game where the position is so simplified that a Class C player would have little chance of losing the position against a Master if both had sufficient thinking time.

Kamikaze-piece. A doomed piece that sells its life for whatever material it can get before capture.

Kingside. The half of the board that includes the files starting with the king and rightward (the e-, f-, g-, and h-files).

Master. A strong player with a United States Chess Federation rating of 2200 or more.

Mate. Same as checkmate, an inescapable attack on the king.

Middlegame. The phase between the opening and the endgame. Most attacks and redeployment of pieces occur here.

Minor pieces. The bishops and knights (as opposed to rooks and queen).

Opening. The beginning of the game, which generally includes the first 10 or so moves. Once the pieces are developed and kings are castled it is properly concluded.

Openings. Established sequences of moves that lead to control of the center and development of the pieces during the early stage of the game.

Passed pawn. A pawn whose advance to the 8th rank (where it could possibly queen) is not opposed by any other pawns who could either block or capture it.

Perpetual check. A sequence of checks that one cannot advantageously escape from. These repeat checks result in draws.

Pin. The prevention of a piece from moving because it would unveil an enemy attack upon a more valuable piece which is shielded behind it. When the shielded piece is the king, the pin is said to be *absolute*, meaning that the pinned piece cannot move. When the more valuable piece is a queen (or other than the king), the attack is said to be *relative*, meaning that the piece can move but it may not be wise to do so.

Plan. A goal or strategy upon which a player bases his moves.

Promotion. The promoting of a pawn to a piece (other than another pawn or king) after it has reached the 8th rank. This increase in power is typically called queening because most players promote to a queen.

Queening. The obtaining of a queen (or, loosely speaking, some other piece) after one's pawn reaches the 8th rank. See promotion.

Queenside. The half of the board that includes the files starting with the queen and leftward (the d-, c-, b-, and a-files).

Rank. A horizontal row of eight squares, designated as 1st rank, 2nd rank, etc.

Rating. A measure of a player's chess playing ability. Ratings range from 0 to 3000 points, with the average rating being 1400 and scholastic players averaging 900 points.

Resign. To give up, ending the chess game. The player simply quits playing, considering his/her position as lost.

Tactics. Maneuvers that take advantage of short-term opportunities, generally involving forks, traps, and pins.

Tempo. Time in chess measured by moves.

Time control. The amount of time each player has to play a specific number of moves or complete the game.

Sacrifice. To voluntary offer material for speculative compensation in material, time, or space.

Smothered mate. Mate delivered by a piece (commonly the knight) when the king is completely boxed in by his own pieces.

Space. The territory controlled by a player or available to him for maneuvers.

Stalemate. The inability move the king without exposing him to check, resulting in a draw. See checkmate.

Zugswang. A German term that means *compulsion to move*. It refers to a situation where a player must move even though it is disadvantageous to do so.

Index

A

active king, 79 – 80
active rook, 145
Alternate, 97, 109, 111, 112, 115, 116, 117 – 121, 123

B

back rank mate, 43
bishops of opposite color, 91
blockade, 83 – 91, 123
boxing the king, 41– 42

C

candidate moves, 55 – 59, 69, 70
castling, 3, 4, 10, 18
castling through check, 4
check, 1, 3, 4, 6 – 10, 12, 14, 15, 27, 43, 46, 48, 60, 61, 63, 67 – 70, 83, 90, 93, 94, 95, 103, 123, 125, 138, 139, 145, 146
checkmate, 1, 6, 42, 46, 47, 50, 123, 124
chess clock, 38, 47, 99, 103 – 104, 106, 107
chess notation
       algebraic, 3, 4, 7 – 10
       descriptive, 7, 14 – 15
club rating, 99 – 100
coach, 41, 59, 61, 75, 92, 97 – 98, 107, 108, 110 – 112, 115, 118, 121
combination, 59, 62, 65 – 70, 123, 140
control of center, 17, 19, 20, 23, 25, 28, 125

D

develop pieces, 17, 19, 20, 21, 23, 26, 28, 32
double attack, 22, 25, 59, 67, 68, 93, 145
draw,8, 46–50, 56, 81, 82, 86–94, 100, 102, 103, 105–107, 110, 111, 123, 145, 146

E

endgame, 37, 41, 42, 47, 76, 79 – 91, 92, 124
en passant, 3, 5, 9, 10, 124

F

H

I

K

M

O

P

Q

qualification, 3, 97 – 103
queen-king mate, 3, 43 – 44
queen-rook mate, 43, 51
queenside, 3, 10, 20, 26, 29, 50, 80, 85, 125, 145

R

rating, 63, 64, 75, 92, 98 – 101, 113, 115, 117, 126, 141
recording moves, 7–10, 99, 106 – 108
rook-king mate, 41 – 43

S

sacrificing, 11, 27, 62, 65, 66, 68, 79, 91, 123, 126, 81, 145
Scholars' Mate, 3, 6, 17, 19, 25 – 31
square of the pawn, 81 – 82, 84
stalemate, 7, 42, 46 – 50, 87, 88, 126, 150
Sudden Death, 47, 103, 104, 105 – 106, 107, 108

T

tactics, 11–13, 63, 64, 66, 83, 126
team captain, 103, 105, 109, 111
technique, 41, 47, 57, 79, 80, 86, 89, 92, 94, 95, 96
three-fold repetition, 7, 8, 102
time forfeit, 104, 105, 106
Top Cop, 59 – 60, 138
Triangle Mate, 44

W

WHY, p. 59-61

Z

zugswang, 80, 126, 132

Appendix

Conducting the Defense
Attacking from Standard Position
Top Cop
Method for Error Reduction and Move Selection
Solutions to Section V, Middlegame: Combinations
Calculating Chess Ratings
Sacrificing for Active Rook Play
Endgame Evaluation (ref. Section VI)
Answers to Endgame Evaluation

Conducting the Defense

In defending, try to remain as flexible as possible while constantly looking for opportunities to counterattack. You don't want to be reduced to passive defense unless there is no other option. Other options to passive defense are: (1) counterattack, (2) exchanging pieces and pawns, and (3) bringing about an endgame. Option three is not much different from option two, excepting that more pieces are traded off. Realize that without counterattack, your passivity may later force you to make some positional concession or cause you to fall into zugswang.

Look for imbalances and seek to capitalize on yours. It may be that your bishop is actually just as strong as your opponent's rook. It might be that simply having more time than your opponent will cause him problems as the defense drags on and time pressure tension increases.

Another critical piece of advice for conducting the defense is to be optimistic. Realize that your opponent can also make mistakes. Try to position yourself to be ready to take advantage of any opportunities. In this regard, try to determine what opportunities may arise during the attacker's continuation of the attack and endeavor to position yourself to counterattack when the moment is right. Realize that for the attacker to finish you off he has to make weakening pawn advances or weaken some other sector by withdrawing pieces from there to concentrate on a target elsewhere. Therefore, see if there are counterattack possibilities in those weakened areas.

Don't act defeated or conduct your defense with a sense of despair. The surest way to be defeated is to think that you already are. Don't continue to agonize about your plight. Do what is necessary for defense and accept it as a necessary evil. Don't waste precious time and energy by continually revisiting the same variations hoping to see something different this time. Try to identify some counterattack measure that you can set to unleash if the attacker gives you a on- or two-move respite while he regroups or tries to bring up more attackers.

Now that you have been advised to remain optimistic and look for counterattack measures, here is a listing of the points that you should consider when conducting defense:

- ♟ Put yourself in your opponent's shoes and try to see his targets of attack.

- ♟ Give yourself as much flexibility as possible while conducting your defense.

- ♟ Be patient.

- ♟ Seek opportunities for counterattack.

- ♟ Seek exchanges.

- ♟ Don't create new weaknesses. Remember that it generally takes two weaknesses to lose.

- ♟ Don't be in a hurry to resign. You can lose only once.

- ♟ Don't act defeated.

ATTACKING FROM THE STANDARD POSITION

1. e4	e5
2. Nf3	Nc6
3. Bc4	Bc5
4. Nc3	Nf6
5. 0-0	0-0
6. d3	d6

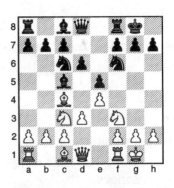

Starting position after 6... d6.

Variation A

7. Be3	Bx3
8. fxe[1]	a6[2]
9. Qe1	Be6!
10. Bb3	Na5
11. Ng4	Nxb
12, axb[3]	c6
13. Qh4	d5?
14. Rxfh6	
15. Rxh!	

Notes to Variation A
1. Note how the pawns control the center. Now White has the open f-file for attack.
2. Planning to attack White's bishop.
3. Note how capturing toward the center strengthens the pawn center.

Variation B

7. Bg5	Be6
8. Nd5	Bxd
9. Bxd	Ne7
10. Bxf	gxf
11. Bb3	Nc6?[1]
12. Nh4	Nd4
13. c3	Nxb
14. Nf4[2]	Kh8
15. axb	d5
16. Qh4	dxe
17. dxe	a6
18. Qh6	Rg
19. Rad	Qf8?
20. Qxf+	Rg7
21. Rd7 followed by R(f)d and Rd8	

Variation B, Game 2

Bg5	a6
Nd5[3]	h6?
Nxf+	gxf
Bxh	Re
Nh4	Na5[4]
Qf3![5]	Kh8
Bxf7	Rg8
Qh5	Bg4
Ng6+	Kh7[6]
Qh4	Rxg6
Bf8+ and mates.	

Notes to Variation B, Games 1 & 2
1. Black should consolidate the kingside (f4, Ng6, Kh8) rather than chase the bishop.
2. Threatening Qg4+ and Qg7 mate.
3. Working on the pinned knight.
4. If 11... Be6, 12. Bxe6 fxe6; 13. Qg4+ Kg7; 14. Qg7++
5. Threatening Qg3 and mate.
6. If 15... Rxg6, 16. Qxg6 Qg8; 17. Qxf6+ Kh7; 18. Bd2 finishes nicely.

Variation B, Game 3

7.	**Bg5**	h6
8.	Bxf	Qxf
9.	Nd5	Qd8
10.	Nd2	Be6
11.	Kh1	a6
12.	f4	Na5
13.	f5	Nxc
14.	dxc	Bd7
15.	Qh5	b5
16.	f6 **Diag.**	gxf
17.	Rxf	c6
18.	Qxh[note]	cxd
19.	Qg5+	Kh7
20.	Rh6 mate	

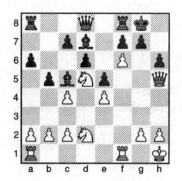

#A.2 After 16. f6 in Game 3 of Variation B.

Note to Game 3: 18. Rxh6 is even stronger.

Alternative Game: **4... Bb4 instead of Bc5.**

1.	e4	e5
2.	Nf3	Nc6
3.	Bc4	Nf6
4.	Nc3	**Bb4**
5.	0-0[1]	0-0[2]
6.	d3	d6
7.	Bg5	h6
8.	Bh4	g5
9.	Nxg!?[3]	hxg
10.	Bxg	Bxc[4]
11.	bxc	Kg7[5]
12.	Qd2[6]	Rh8[7]
13.	f4	Qg8[8]
14.	fxe	Ne8
15.	Rxf+ and wins.	

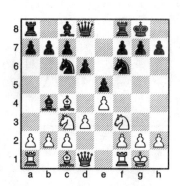

#A.3. The Bb4 line after 6th move.

Notes for Bb4 Alternative:

1. White dares Black to capture the knight and try to win the e-pawn.
2. Black does not blunder. If 5 ... Bxc; 6. dxc Nxe; 7. Bd5, 7. Qd5, or 7. Re1 is strong.

135

3. This sacrifice is very dangerous and likely decisive against weak defense.

4. Black keeps White from playing Nd5 and winning immediately.

5. If 11... Be6?; 12. f4! Bxc4 13. fxe wins convincingly. The computer Fritz recommends 11... d5;12. exd5 Na5; 13.Qf3 Kg7; 14.Rae1 Qd6; 15.Bxf6+ Qxf6; 16.Qg3+ Kh6; 17. Rxe5 but Black's future is still very grim.

6. Threatening 13. Bh6+ and either 14. Qg5+ or 14. Bxf8(?). However, computer evaluation suggests as even stronger the immediate 12. f4.

7. If 12 ... Kg6, 13. Bh4! with Qg5+ wins.

8. If 13 ... R-h5; 14. fxe5 Nxe; 15. Bxf6+ wins easily.

Reminder: Don't neglect thoroughly reading *Aggressive Opening Play* from page 32. That valuable chapter introduces you to two commonly occurring attack schemes: the Center Fork Trick and the Fried Liver Attack. From Diag. A.4 below, either White attacks with Ng5 (going for a Fried Liver Attack) or Black can enter the Center Fork Trick if White protects his e-pawn with Nc3 as in Diag. A.5.

#A.4 An early crisis point.

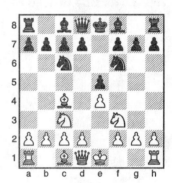
#A.5 Black can play 4... Nxe5.

If the Center Fork Trick is so desirable for Black, is there a version of it that White can play? Yes! If Black tries to play a Petroff Defense with 2... Nf6 rather than defend his pawn with Nc6 (see Diag. A6 of next page), then White can attempt to direct play into a Center Fork Trick position by playing 3. Nc6, giving Diag. A.7. Black will likely enter the Four Knights Defense by replying with 3... Nc6 (Diag. A.8). Now we introduce a finesse. Instead of playing 4. Bc4 – allowing the fork – we play 4. a3, which encourages Black to bring his bishop out to c5 and, thus, allow White to play the Center Fork Trick with an extra tempo!

136

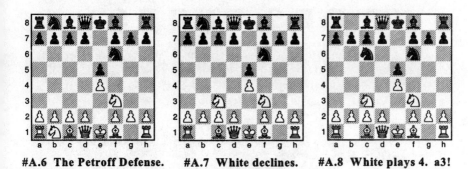

#A.6 The Petroff Defense.   #A.7 White declines.   #A.8 White plays 4. a3!

T O P   C O P
S T O P S   F L O P S

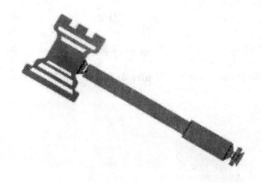

THREATS
What does his move threaten? What threats did he give me?

Opponent's doings

PLANS
Is his move part of a plan? Was my original plan affected?
What is my plan?

CHECKS/CAPTURES
Do I have any forcing moves, such as checks and captures?

Our doings

PATTERNS
Are there any thematic patterns emerging, such as mating
setups or file control?

Method for Error Reduction and Move Selection

Respond to threats

What is attacked? (If there is a threat, process candidates moves.*)
What might be the planned attack?

Seek own threats

Are there any captures already present? (If there is, process candidate moves.*)
Are there any checks or direct attacks?
Are there any unprotected pieces? (If so, how might I exploit them.*)
Are there any threats or patterns that can be prepared?

Improve position

Are there any positional aspects (imbalances) to consider?

- ♟ material balance
- ♟ the initiative (controlling the game or making threats);
- ♟ pawn structure (doubled, isolated, passed, etc.)
- ♟ space (control of more territory in a sector)
- ♟ lead in development (a time advantage)
- ♟ play on files, diagonals, and key squares
- ♟ superior pieces, especially knights versus bishops

Are there any weak points that may need defense?
Are there any pieces that can be made more effective?

* Process candidate moves:

(1) Select candidate moves (generally three or more) to review
(2) Evaluate the selected moves
(3) Choose a move to make

Solutions to Section VI, Middlegame: Combinations

Diagram 5.5
1. Nd5   Qd8
2. Nd4!   fxg
3. Nc6 wins queen.

Diagram 5.6
1. Qh5   Qxh
2. Ne7+   Kh7
3. Rxh++

Diagram 5.7
1. Qxc+   bxc
2. Ba6++

Diagram 5.8
1. Re8+   Bd8
2. Rxd+   Rxd
3. Nc7+   Kb8
4. Na6+   Ka8
5. Qb8+   Rxb
6. Nc7++

Diagram 5.9
1. Qxf+   Rxf
2. Re8++

Diagram 5.10
1. Rxb   Qxb
2. Qxg+   Kd8
3. Qxb

Diagram 5.11
1. Rc8   Rxc
2. Qe7   Qc6
3. d8-queen+
(or 1... Qxd; 2. Qf8+)

Diagram 5.12
1. Bxh+   Kxh
2. Ng5+   Kg6
3. Qd3+ or 3. Qg4

Diagram 5.13
1. Qxh+   Bxh
2. Rxh+   Kg7

3. R-h7+   Kxf
4. Rxf++

Diagram 5.14
1. Qg4+   Bg7
2. Bxf   any
3. Qxg++

Diagram 5.15
1. Nh6+   Kh8
2. Nf7+   Kg8
3. Nxd

Diagram 5.16
1. Be4   Qxe
2. Qxf+   Kg8
3. Qg7++

Diagram 5.17
1. Qc6   bxc
2. bxc   Kb8
3. R(f)-a1   any
4. Ra8++

Diagram 5.18
1. Nf5+   Bxf
2. Rh4+   Nh5
3. Rh5++

Diagram 5.19
1. Be8   Bf5
2. exf   R(a)xe
3. Qxg+   Kh8
4. Qh5+   Bh6
5. Qxh++

Diagram 5.20
1. Rxb+   Bxb
2. Rd7+   Ne7
3. Rxe+   Kg8
4. Ne6   any
5. Rg7++

Diagram 5.21
1. Nxf+   Bxf
2. d5 winning a knight
      or bishop

Diagram 5.22
1. Nxf+   Bxf
2. Qe4   g6
3. Qxa

Diagram 5.23
1. Bxh+   Kxh
2. Qxh+   Kg8
3. Bxg   Kxg
4. Qg4+   Kh7
5. Rf3

Diagram 5.24
1. h7+   Kf8
2. Bb4! The cross-pin
      wins.

Diagram 5.25
1. Rxe   Rxe
2. g3!   f4
3. g4!
or 2... g4; 3. Kf2

Diagram 5.26
1. Qxf   Bxf
2. Nh6++

Diagram 5.27
1. g4   h5
2. Kg3   hxg
3. Kxh

Diagram 5.28
1. Qxd   Rxd
2. Re8+   Kd7
3. Rd8+   Kc6
4. Rxd

How to Calculate Ratings

In the first publication of this book, I demonstrated how ratings were calculated by the USCF and presented some examples. Since then, the rating structure employed by the USCF has undergone significant changes to accommodate the explosion of scholastic chess and the influence that such unrated newcomers were having on the rating system. In June of 2008 the USCF adopted a new model that could handle these fluctuations more effectively. Though there is an approximation of this complex structure that laymen can use, there is no longer any need to personally calculate the ratings as the USCF's Rating Estimator can always be accessed online.

So I'm just going to give a few explanations about their systems so that you can better understand it and briefly explain it to your players. Most basically, the formula – used by the USCF – for calculating rating changes is based on the probability of your winning against an opponent with a given rating higher or lower than yours. For example, a player rated 400 points above you is expected to win 91% of the time. Therefore if he wins the game– as expected – he would gain only 2 points; but if you win the game, you would get 34 points. And even if you "only" tied the game, you will still get 16 points.

Provisionally-rated Players

Since beginning players will likely be unrated, their initial rating will be provisional. Ratings are considered provisional for players who have played 25 or fewer games (rather than 20 under the old system), and established if having played more than 25 games. There are two different formulas to compute ratings. The criterion for using the different formulas depends on whether the player has completed 8 tournament games. Either the "special" rating formula or the "standard" formula is used depending upon whether a player has completed 8 tournament games or fewer. Of course, established ratings are based on the standard formula.

Another factor that puzzles those who first sees the USCF rating formula is the K-factor. This variable represents the largest change that your rating can experience as a result of the game and is an estimate of player rating volatility. The higher the value, the more uncertain the prior rating is assumed to be, and, therefore, how rapidly a player's rating may change. Its value is determined from the number of prior games, the number of games played in the current event, and the prior rating.

For established players versus established player, the value K=32 is generally used. If you're playing a provisional player, the factor K is scaled by n/25, where n is one plus the number of games your opponent has played. This formula has the property that if both players are established then the sum of the rating changes is zero. It turns out that if the rating difference is more than 719 points, then if the strong player wins, there is no change in either players' ratings. Note that during the provisional period, *beating* a player whose rating is more than 400 points below your rating can actually *decrease* your rating. This is a consequence of the averaging process. This very significant tweak to the rating system prevents a player who, after one game, has obtained an inflated provisional rating trying to win 24 more games against much weaker opposition and obtaining a high established rating.

Rating Considerations and Levels

The below table gives a rough approximation of ratings for established players with no bonus point considerations. Keep in mind that change in how the USCF applies the K-factor allows the points exchanged to exceed 32.

Rating Difference	Lower-Rated Wins	Higher-Rated Wins
50	22	10
100	24	9
150	27	7
200	29	6
250	30	5
300	32	4
350	33	3
400	34	2
500	36	2

There is more to the USCF's rating formula than the k-factor. Bonus points are also awarded for exceptional performance in a tournament. The combination of these new modifications are useful in dealing with provisional players wildly fluctuating ratings and strength gains. The new system gives a better estimate of the player's real strength once they obtain their established rating.

Notwithstanding the correction to ratings, playing much higher-rated opponents is still the best method of getting a high provisional rating and, consequently, an established rating. Of course you will actually have to upset a few of your higher-rated opponents in this process! Anyway, take it as an opportunity when you get the chance to sit in front of a higher-rated opponent.

While speaking of higher-rated opponents, let me give you a very valuable piece of advice: **play the board, not the person**. Don't worry about your opponent's rating or who they are – play the position on the chess board.

You should regard your rating as only a tool to help you chart your progress. Remember that provisional ratings vary over a wide range and, hence, cannot be relied upon. Too, established ratings are not an absolute criteria of strength, especially if the player is rusty or has been seriously studying but not playing in over-the-board competition.

Remember that the only thing that matters when you play is **how well you play the present game**. Ratings are a historical measure that do vary from game to game. The guy might have beat you twenty times before, but it is certainly no guarantee that he will beat you this game!

What of grandmasters? Grandmasters are titled players. Masters become grandmasters by competing in qualifying tournaments. When the master achieves three or more grandmaster norms based on the strength of the tournaments while competing against other international masters, he is awarded the title. Usually grandmaster ratings range from 2400 to 2800.

See the chart on the following page to see the varies categories of chess classes and their rating range.

143

Chart of USCF Titles and Ratings

Title	Rating
Senior Master	2400 and Up
Master	2200 - 2399
Expert	2000 - 2199
Class A	1800 - 1999
Class B	1600 - 1799
Class C	1400 - 1599
Class D	1200 - 1399
Class E	1000 - 1199
Class F	800 - 999
Class G	600 - 799
Class H	400 - 599
Class I	200 - 399
Class J	Under 200

Sacrificing for Active Rook Play
(Illustration of Principle 8 of *Endgame Principles*, Sect. VI)

White has the active rook and the better-placed king. If Black relies on passive defense, White will win in due time by walking over to the queenside

St. Petersburg vs. London
Black to move.

and winning the rook pawn with a double attack. Rather than allow this turn of events, Black immediate goes on the counter attack by activating his rook at the cost of the pawn.

1. ... Rc6!; 2. Rxa5 Rc4+ Now Black has two immediate gains: (a) his rook is actively placed, and (b) White's king has been driven from its aggressive post. **3. Ke3** Trying to remain as active as possible. **3. ... Kf7!** Black now takes the time out to improve his king's position. **4. Ra8 Kg7; 5. a5 Ra4!** *Rooks belong behind passed pawns.* **6. a6 Kh6!** Trying to reach g5, where the king would be both free from checks and able to attack White's pawns. **7. f4 g5!; 8. fxg+** If 8. f5, then not 8. ... Rxg?; 9. a7 Ra4; 10. Rh8+ Kg7; 11. a=queen. To draw, 8. ... Kg7 is necessary. **8. ... fxg; 9. Kd3 Kg7!** By keeping his king at g7 and h7 and keeping his rook

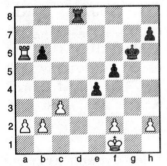

Tarrasch vs. Rubinstein
Black to move.

attacking the pawn or checking the king away from attempts at protecting it, Black assures the draw.

This second diagram shows another position where passive defense is not practical. So Black immediately activates his rook: **1 ... Rd2!; 2. Rxb+ Kg5** Now Black's plan is clear. He hopes to construct a mating net around the White king with f4-f3. Realizing that his king is in danger and that Black can almost force a draw – at the least! – White tries to improve his king's position. **3. Ke1 Rc2; 4. Rb5!** (No better is a4-a5-a6.) **Kg4!; 5. h3+!** White can't allow f4 followed by Kf3, when he is on the verge of losing. **5... Kxh; 6. Rxf Rxb; 7. Rf4 Rxa; 8. Rxe h5** *Passed pawns must be pushed as soon as feasible!* **9. c4 Kg2; 10. Rf4**

145

Rc2; **11. Rh4 Kf3; 12. Kd1 Rxf; 13. c5 Ke3; 14. Rxh Kd4** and the draw was had because of Black's decision to activate his rook.

In 1910, Lasker gave us another excellent example of sacrificing a pawn for active defense in his championship match against Schlechter. In the below diagram, Black is in a little trouble. White is threatening to capture the f-pawn with c4 followed by Kf4. Even worst, his king is not participating in the fight. Lasker could try passive defense with 54... Ra1, but computer analysis with Fritz11 shows that his game-time decision was accurate:

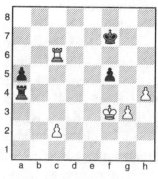

Schlechter – E. Lasker
Black to make 54th move.

54...Re4!? Lasker opts for active defense rather than playing Ra1. **55.Rc5 Kf6; 56.Rxa5 Rc4** Now it is White who is thrown on the defensive! Note that Black's king also has more possibilities, able to shift from the 3rd to the 4th rank. Fritz's evaluation has plummeted from 2.6 to a mere 0.8. **57.Ra6+ Ke5; 58.Ra5+ Kf6; 59.Ra6+ Ke5; 60.Ra5+ Kf6; 61.Ra2 Ke5** Threatening to drive the king back with Rc6+ and perhaps further penetrating with Ke4. **62.Rb2 Rc3+; 63.Kg2 Kf6** Black keeps the h-pawn in check and really could not have safely advanced, anyway. (63...Ke4 64.Rb4+ Ke3 65.Rb3!) **64.Kh3 Rc6; 65.Rb8** White abandons the pawn, seeing no way to make progress. **65...Rxc2; 66.Rb6+ Kg7; 67.h5 Rc4; 68.Rg6+ Kh7; 69.Rf6** The game score gives **69... Ra4** and a draw. But it is obvious that Rc5 forcibly holds the draw. For instance: 69...Rc5 70.Kh4 (70.Kg2 Kg7 71.Rg6+ Kf7 72.Kf3 Rc4 73.Rd6 Kg7 74.Ra6 Rg4 75.Rb6 Rg5 76.h6+ Kh7 77.Rf6 Rg8) 70...Rc4+ 71.Kg5 Rg4+ ½–½

The rook is the clumsiest defender of all the pieces. Hence you often can fare better giving up a pawn to activate it. Be careful trying to apply this strategy with the minor pieces, though! Moreover, if you aren't sure how to conduct this active defense, then cling to your pawns until your technique (endgame skills) matures.

Endgame Evaluation

This skill's evaluation includes queening maneuvers, rook-handling skills such as the Lucena and Philidor position, pawn promotion, square of the pawn, and other commonly occurring themes.

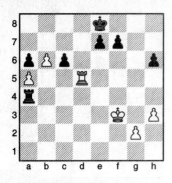

#A.12 White to queen.

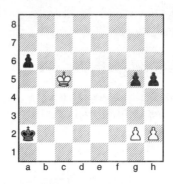

#A.13 Black to use his passer.

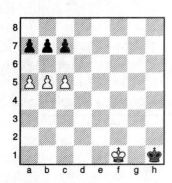

#A.14 White breaks through.

#A.15 Draw or win—whoever moves?

#A.16 Use of the opposition.

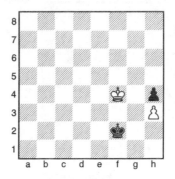

#A.17 Black to Draw.

#A.18 White uses a known queening tactic to win.

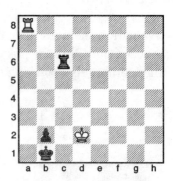

#A.19 How does Black win?

#A.20 White to use Philidor's drawing method.

#A.21 Black to move and win.

#A.22 Black to move and win.

#A.23 White to move and win.

148

#A.24 How should Black *seek* a draw?

#A.25 White to move and win.

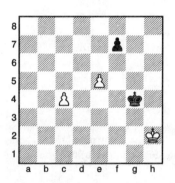

#A.26 White to move and win.

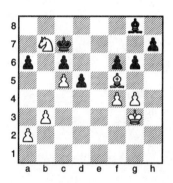

#A.27 Which piece should White save–and why?

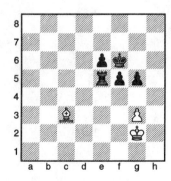

#A.28 White to move and eventually win.

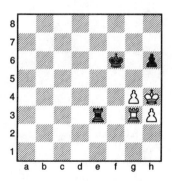

#A.29 Black to move and draw.

149

Answers to *Endgame Evaluation*

Diag. A.12
1. Rb5!   cxb
2. b7 and queens.

Diag. A.13

1.	...	Kb3
2.	Kb6	Kc3
3.	Kxa	Kd3
4.	Kb5	Ke3
5.	Kc5	Kf2 eating pawns

and queening.

Diag. A.14
1. b6   axb
2. c6!   bxc
3. a6 and queens.

Diag. A.15
With correct play this position is drawn regardless of who moves:
1. Ke6   Ke8
2. f7+   Kf8
3. Kf6 stalemate, or
1. ...   Kf7!
2. Ke5   Kf8!
3. Ke6   Ke8 with the opposition

Diag. A.16
1. Ka5 (or Kc5) Kb7
2. a8=Q+   Kxa;
3. Ka6   Kb8
4. b7   Kc7
5. Ka7   Kd7;
6. b8=Q.

Diag. A.17
1. ...   Ke2!
2. Kb4   Ke3
3. Kxh   Kf4
4. Ka5   Kf5 and eventual stalemate – by either side!

Diag. A.18
1. Rh8   Rxa
2. Rh7+   K any
3. Rxa.

Diag. A.19
1. ...   Rd7+
2. Ke2   Rd5!
3. Ra7   Kc2
4. Rc7+   Kb3
5. Rb7+   Kc3
6. Rc7+   Kb4
7. Rb7+   Rb5!

Diag. A.20
1. Rd8   Kg3
2. Rg8+   Kf4
3. Rf+   Ke3
4. Re+   Kd3
5. Rf8   Ke4
6. Re8+ and more checks.

Diag. A.21
1. ...   g5! and White cannot capture the g-pawn without stepping outside the square of the f-pawn.

Diag. A.22
1. ...   a5!
2. Kc4   a4! and Black wins.

Diag. A.23
1. b4!   Kc4;
2. b6 and queens.

Diag. A.24
1. ...   f3
2. Qxf   f2
3. Qg4+   Kh2
4. Qf3   Kg1
5. Qg3+   Kh1! aiming for stalemate.

Diag. A.25
1. Kg3!   Qf3+!?
2. Kxf!   Kh1
3. Qg2++.

Diag. A.26
1. e6!   fxe
2. c5   Kf5
3. c6   Ke5
4. c7   Kd6
5. c8=Q.

Diag. A.27
1. Nd6!   gxf
2. Nxf   Kd7
3. Nd4 and wins because of having the
better minor piece.

Diag. A.28
1. Kf3   g4+
2. Kf4   Kf7
3. Kxe5
and if
1. Kf3   f4
2. g4!

Diag. A.29
1. ...   Rxg
2. Kxg   h5!
3. Kh4   hxg
4. hxg   Kg6 and draws easily.